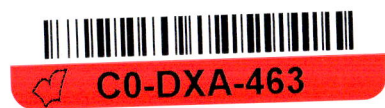

Breaking the Curses of Slavery
Prayers for African-Americans

Pamela Burgess Main

Cover Designed by Erin Katherine Main

For more copies, visit www.lulu.com

Copyright © 2013 by Pamela Burgess Main

All rights reserved.

Produced in the United States of America

Unless written permission to reprint is secured,
reproduction by any medium, including electronic,
is strictly prohibited.

For permission, contact: breakingthecursesofslavery@gmail.com

ISBN 978-1-304-68050-1 (sc)

"I am the Lord your God,
Who brought you out of the land of Egypt,
Out of the house of slavery....
You shall not make for yourself an idol....
For I the Lord your God am a jealous God,
Punishing children for the iniquity of parents,
To the <u>third</u> and the <u>fourth</u> generation of those who reject Me,
But showing steadfast love to the thousandth generation
Of those who love Me and keep My commandments."

Exodus 20: 2-6 (NRSV)

This Book is dedicated to our President, Barack Obama, who has set a historic precedence as the Commander in Chief of the United States of America.
Please join in prayer, asking the Lord for the continual protection and well-being of our First Family, in the name of Jesus. Amen.

CONTENTS

PREFACE..ix

The Top Ten

1. COMING THROUGH THE WRONG PORTALS.. 1
2. BEING STOLEN... 3
3. BEING SOLD... 6
4. BEING BOUGHT.. 8
5. THE BAD THAT WAS BROUGHT OVER FROM AFRICA................... 11
6. WORSHIPING DEITIES FROM AFRICA... 15
7. THE GOOD THAT WAS BROUGHT OVER FROM AFRICA............... 34
8. DISHONORING GOD... 36
9. COLONIZATION.. 37
10. NATIONAL FEAR.. 39

The Rest

11. A BAD PARTNER.. 41
12. ABANDONMENT... 43
13. ABUSE.. 45
14. ADULTERY... 47
15. AGAINST US PROFITING FROM OUR AGRICULTURE................... 49
16. ALCOHOLISM... 50
17. ALWAYS NEEDING A VILLIAN IN MY LIFE.................................... 51
18. AM I BLACK ENOUGH?.. 53
19. ANIMOSITY BEWTEEN FATHERS and THEIR CHILDREN.............. 54
20. ANIMOSITY BETWEEN MOTHERS and THEIR CHILDREN............ 56
21. ANXIETY.. 58
22. APATHY... 59

23. BAD BANKING and MORTGAGES.. 60
24. BAD BUSINESS 61
25. BAD EDUCATION 63
26. BAD HOUSING 65
27. BAD INVESTMENTS 67
28. BAD MARRIAGES.. 68
29. BAD MEDICINE.. 70
30. BEING A BULLY... 72
31. BEING A CRUEL TASK MASTER... 73
32. BEING A FATHER WHO ABANDONS.. 74
33. BEING A MOTHER WHO ABANDONS.. 76
34. BEING ABANDONED BY YOUR FATHER.. 78
35. BEING ABANDONED BY YOUR MOTHER...................................... 79
36. BEING ATTACKED... 81
37. BEING BULLIED... 82
38. BEING CALLED A NIGGER or OTHER RACIST NAMES.................. 84
39. BEING PLAYED or TRICKED or USED.. 85
40. BETRAYING YOUR OWN PEOPLE.. 87
41. BEING RIPPED OFF.. 89
42. THE BLAME GAME.. 91
43. BROKEN PROMISES and CAUGHT IN THE CROSSFIRE................. 92

44. COMPLAINING... 93
45. THE COON... 95
46. CRABS IN A BARREL... 96

47. DEPRESSION	97
48. DISTRACTIONS	98
49. ENTERTAINMENT MEDIA'S RACIST STEREOTYPES	99
50. ENTITLEMENT TO OVER-EAT	100
51. EXCESSIVENESS	102
52. EXPLOSIVE ANGER	103
53. FAT GENE	104
54. FEAR OF FAILURE	105
55. FEELING LIKE YOU NEVER PLEASE YOUR PARENTS	106
56. FINANCES BEING MISHANDLED	107
57. FOOD	108
58. HATERS	110
59. HIDDEN AGENDAS	111
60. HUMILIATION OF BEING UNEMPLOYED or RETIRED	112
61. INACCESSIBILITY TO ACCESS CODES	114
62. INJURIES and NEAR DEATH EXPERIENCES WITH KIDS	115
63. JEALOUSY	116
64. JIM CROW	118
65. LACK OF OPPORTUNITY FOR OUR BLACK YOUTH	120
66. LEECHES (FOLKS THAT PREY)	121
67. LETTING EVIL SPIRITS IN	123
68. LOSS OF CHILDREN	124
69. MAMMY (FOR OVER-WEIGHT WOMEN)	125
70. NEGATIVE IMAGERY and RACIAL SLURS	127
71. NIGGA JAILS and HOLDING CELLS	130
72. NOT BEING MARRIED	131
73. NOT GETTING ENOUGH CREDIT	132
74. NOT LOOKING FOR US, WHEN WE GO MISSING	134
75. NOT RELEASING PEOPLE WHO ARE JEALOUS OF YOU	135
76. OUR FOUNDING FATHERS	136
77. PEDOPHILIA (SEXUAL CHILD ABUSE)	139
78. PERSONAL FEAR	141
79. PIMPING and BEING PIMPED	143
80. PROCRASTINATION	144
81. PROSTITUTION	145
82. RACIAL HIERARCHY	146
83. SELF-DESTRUCTION	149
84. SELF-DESTRUCTIVE GUILT	150
85. SELF-DESTRUCTION ONCE I'VE MADE IT	151
86. SELF-PITY	152
87. SERVANTS SEEN and NOT HEARD	153
88. SEXUAL SIN	154
89. SKIN COLOR WAR	160
90. STAYING IN YOUR PLACE	161

91. UNEMPLOYMENT FOR THE FAMILY	162
92. UNEMPLOYMENT FOR ME	163
93. UNFAIR EMPLOYERS	164
94. UNFAIR COURT SYSTEMS	165
95. UNFAIR WAGES	168
96. VANITY	169
97. VOODOO	171
98. VIOLENCE	173
99. WOMEN HANGING ON YOUR MAN	175
100. THE BLESSING OF CONQUERING OUR ENEMIES	176

PREFACE

``` I was introduced to the concept of breaking generational curses by Dr. Paul Cox. Through his books and courses, I've come to understand that Jesus Christ has actually given us the authority to stand in the wake of our family's generational sin, and break off any and all curses committed by our ancestors.

Dr. Cox and his ministry have already published a book called, "Prayers For Generational Deliverance". My book is meant to be a supplement to his. My book is not a blueprint on how to effectively eliminate generational curses off family lines, but a guide and a framework, to help begin the spiritual healing of that which has plagued black families for so many years. The incessant alcoholism, sexual addiction, poverty, discrimination, lack of education, incarceration and so forth, that may have been initiated by one family member and then passed down the family line, through constant re-introduction by other family members. By basically canceling generational curses, through the simple renunciation and forgiveness of those family members by prayer, brings spiritual release and spiritual healing to generational issues, through Christ.

(To the reader) YOU KNOW MORE THAN I DO! Here's what you know. Thousands and thousands of people make up your generational line. Here's also what you know.
Of those thousands, someone in your family line was likely to offend God at some point, thus bringing curses on themselves and bringing those curses on to other members of your family, generationally. Biblically, a curse is reinstated in a family line, every four years. See Paul Cox's notes.

However, Jesus Christ allows us to break each and every curse by the authority of His name, by a simple act of prayer and forgiveness. Amazing!

Now we can all obtain spiritual freedom from things that have plagued our families for so long. In the name of Jesus, we can cancel, cut, and break off any and all curses through praying specifically about that curse and calling it to leave in the name of Christ. By repenting to God on behalf of our ancestors, we can begin to experience relief in our lives, as well as our children's and grandchildren's lives.

We serve an Awesome God, Who's willing and ready to rid us of generational curses, that may not have been caused by us, but now can be laid to rest once and for all. Part of this prayer exercise is to jog your memory of past acts that you or your family members experienced. The hope is to bring forgiveness and closure to these incidences, for your sake and your family's sake.

Sometimes, you will notice that in the middle of a prayer, I will start calling on a certain emotion to leave. For example, "doubt leave, anger leave". These are some of the emotions that Dr. Cox teaches, that I sense welling up when certain curses are being removed. Certain emotional ties need to be commanded to leave, so spiritual healing can fully occur. The emotions I command to leave, may not be the
```

emotions you are feeling when you pray. But whatever negative emotion(s) you are feeling, be sure to tell it to leave, in the name of Jesus.

Remember, my prayers are simply a template (examples) on how to pray over various curses. Nothing is set in stone. If you are praying, and find you are being led down a different path, please pray your way and clean out all those things God brings to mind in freeing your family tree. Also please add your own personal history and information to the prayers when you say them. I don't know everything. I understand I've missed key facts. Every personal, historical, or legal fact you add, just makes your prayers stronger.

Also, it is imperative to understand, that I am not saying, that everything bad in our life, is a curse. Sometimes LIFE is just hard. And the lots we've been given to live are simply a twist of life. Some things in life are truly out of our control. But we can count on a good God to help us navigate through it. Say you've been given a bad hand in life, and you really don't feel you're cursed in any way. Surely not all of our ancestors in Africa were necessarily cursed people when they were abducted. However, the outcome of that history still plagues us today. Not everyone came out of slavery whole. These are prayers of forgiveness and healing, to help us move on. If you feel you are not cursed, but you want to pray parts of these prayers, be honest with God and say to Him, "Lord, I don't think I'm cursed in this area, but there is definitely something up. Would You show me how to pray about this?" And let the Lord show you how to pray about it.

You may find parallels in the prayers. It may seem like repetitiveness, but some points will be hit again and again, at various angles, until those points are eradicated from your family lines. Words like shame, anger, etc, will crop up again and again. But don't be discouraged or dismayed. A lot went down in the almost 400 years of developing the African-American race, and there's a lot of unpacking to do, in order to get rid of the bad stuff. We're also unpacking what drives us to do the unhealthy things we do now and hopefully, to set us free to live the life God intended us to enjoy since the beginning of His creation.

As you begin to pray, you will begin to see an avalanche of atrocities that bombarded our past and present. The exciting thing is, NOW, we can change our future. We don't have to be spiritually, physically, mentally, or emotionally bound to the "curses" in our lives, our parents' lives, our grandparents' lives, or our slave ancestors' lives.

Many of our people are already free from the bondage of our forefathers. But there were and are, too many offenses that still keep us down. There is no harm in allowing our Lord and Savior to sweep clean the unseen baggage that's been carried by our families for hundreds of years.

Some of us have a few patterns that we recognize in our lives, which could be a result of a generational curse. Get rid of it, with the help of the Lord Jesus. The process is *so simple*. But don't be fooled. None of the power that you're asking for to remove the curses, can be done, without the AWESOME power of Jesus Christ.

He did miracles while He was on the earth, and He's doing them today. All prayers are conducted by asking the Lord Jesus to remove and restore. No exceptions. Christ is the Mover and Restorer in this process.

Sometimes you will come across a line in a prayer and say to yourself, that doesn't apply to me. Then don't say the line. Pray only what <u>applies</u> to you.

Sometimes you will come across a line in a prayer, and you'll be moved to pray for things that aren't written on the page. Or, you will feel led to pray about something, that's not in your personal memory. Do it. Give everything to Jesus, as it comes up. You can trust Him.

Sometimes, when I'm praying and something else comes up that I don't understand, I'll say, "Lord, I'm feeling this or I'm seeing that. I don't understand, but I give it all to You, and if anyone in my generational line participated in this, I ask for Your forgiveness. If anyone in my generational line was a victim of this, I choose to forgive this and ask You to bring healing to my family line."

In saying the prayers, there is often (if not always) asking and giving forgiveness. This is also the key to unlocking the curses. In my experience, asking for forgiveness is not contingent on feelings. It's based purely on will. Your will.

What I'm trying to say is the Lord (He is so awesome) is not expecting us to feel positive about the negative issues we are bringing to Him. I recommend when the emotions you are feeling are overwhelming, that you give every emotion to God, as you pray. It sounds like this, "Lord I wish to forgive ____. Lord I give You my fear in doing this. I give You my anger, my sadness, my helplessness, etc."

If the issue is too much to bear, your prayer can sound like this, "Lord, I don't want to do this, but I CHOOSE to forgive ____." Often when we do this, I find the Lord moves, as we give our wills over to Him. I love this! The Lord doesn't expect us to be superheroes, but He wants to help. His love is so amazing, that He will not violate our wills. But the second we turn our wills over to Him, by choosing to forgive, He can begin the healing process in us, and in our family line.

Remember. Some prayers, or lines in prayers will <u>not</u> apply to you or your situation, so don't say them. But if you come across a prayer or line that does apply, even if it's a little embarrassing…say it! Get that hardship off your chest and be free of it.

It's complicated. Some of us have not only African blood, but white slave masters' blood pumping in our veins. Some of our ancestors were sold by the very Africans they lived among. Some of our family members were lynched, branded, sold, traded, whipped, beaten, raped, incarcerated, kept illiterate, deprived, over-medicated, underpaid, and yes, there was that little thing called slavery.

The thing is, not all of us bounced back from the atrocities we went through in this country. In some ways, we are still victims.

Some of the negative things that our forefathers and mothers endured, got passed down our generational line. The Good News is, we have the ability through Jesus Christ, to eradicate the curses placed on our lives!

The prayer steps to remove family curses can look like this:

1. Acknowledge God and Jesus as Lord, saying:
   "Lord God, or Father God, or Lord Jesus"

2. Identify yourself as a representative of the family, saying:
   "As a member of the ____ family, I stand before You Lord"

3. Bring before God the curse, asking Him to remove it, saying:
   "I ask You Lord to please remove the curse of ____ from my family line"

4. By your authority as a family member, break the curse, saying:
   "By the power that is invested in me, I cut, sever, and break all ties to the curse of ____ off my family line."

5. Acknowledge the Power of Jesus (in His name and by His Blood)
   "...by the blood of Jesus Christ of Nazareth or in the name of Jesus...."

6. Ask God to forgive the original family sinner and sin that brought the curse on the family line

7. Now you forgive them

8. Name every family member that you know of, that participated in the sin (including yourself if it applies), asking God to forgive them and their actions

9. Now you forgive each family member and their actions (even if you don't feel like it). When it becomes too painful to forgive them, say:
   "Lord, I don't want to forgive this family member, but I choose to forgive them"

10. Any bad emotions connected with the events, you give to God, saying:
    "God, I give You my sadness. I give You my anger. I give You my guilt. I give You my shame." Or command them to leave, "Sadness, leave. Anger, leave."

11. Ask the Lord for restoration, saying:
    "Lord, please restore all that has been taken from our family line..."

12. Always close your prayer, saying:
    "In the name of Jesus."
    It is only through His power that we are able to remove the curses.

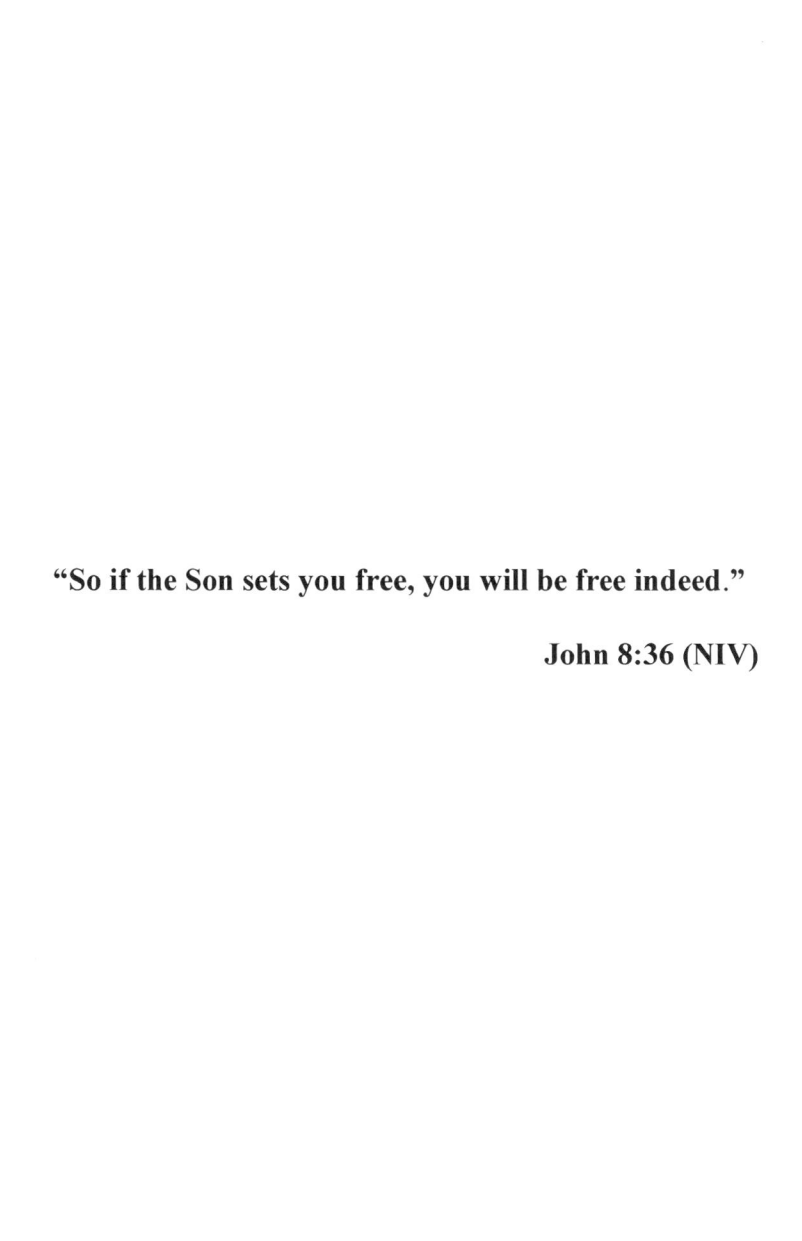

"So if the Son sets you free, you will be free indeed."

John 8:36 (NIV)

1. COMING THROUGH THE WRONG PORTALS

Father, in the name of Jesus Christ of Nazareth,
I come before Your throne, humbly. Due to incredibly historical events, I am here, standing before You, in the United States of America.

Unlike other nationalities that came to this country, the portal through which my ancestors initially entered this land, was NOT voluntary, or seeking a future of hope, freedom, or prosperity. In fact Lord, the portal my family line came through, was the portal of captivity, enslavement, and oppression. We came to this country through the wrong door, Lord God.

So I ask You Lord, in the name of Jesus, to please remove the curse of coming through the wrong portals into this country, off my family line and off every other African-American family line in this country.

As a member of my family line, I ask You Lord to please re-route our entry points, letting me exit and close all the slave trade portals through which our ancestors arrived.

By the power invested in me as a representative of my family line, I cut, sever, and break all ties to the curse off my family line, of coming through the wrong portals to this country, by the blood of Jesus Christ.

In the name and power of Jesus of Nazareth, I choose to exit and close all slave trade ports, portals, gateways, and doors that my ancestors entered; including the following seaports, rivers, trails, holding containers, and markets:

New Orleans, I close your portal, in the name of Jesus.
Biloxi, I close your portal, in the name of Jesus.
Savannah, I close your portal, in the name of Jesus.
St. Helena, I close your portal, in the name of Jesus.
Charleston, I close your portal, including Sullivan's Island where slaves were first unloaded , processed, and groomed for sales, in the name of Jesus.
Annapolis, I close your portal, in the name of Jesus.
New York, I close your portal, in the name of Jesus.
Newport Rhode Island, I close your portal, in the name of Jesus.
Boston, I close your portal, in the name of Jesus.

Manchester Dock, I close your portal, in the name of Jesus.
Richmond, Virginia, I close your portal, in the name of Jesus.
Rappahannock River, Virginia, I close your portal, in the name of Jesus.
York River, Virginia, I close your portal, in the name of Jesus.
South Potomac River, I close your portal, in the name of Jesus.
Upper and Lower James River, I close your portals, in the name of Jesus.
Any other U.S. ports, I close your portals, in the name of Jesus.

Any illegal U.S. ports through which my ancestors may have been smuggled, I close your portals in the name of Jesus.

I choose to forgive the following regional entries, in the name of Jesus of Nazareth:

I choose to forgive the transporting of 210, 000 slaves to the Carolinas/Georgia
I choose to forgive the transporting of 128,000 slaves to the Chesapeake region
I choose to forgive the transporting of 27,000 slaves to the Northern US
I choose to forgive the transporting of 22,000 slaves to the Gulf Coast

I ask Lord that You would forgive all those involved in trading my family as slaves. As a representative of this family, I choose to forgive all those involved in the kidnapping, detaining, transporting, and selling of my family members.

I cancel all captivity, enslavement, and oppression off my family line. I close the doors and declare my family members free from being hostages.

In the name of Jesus, I declare the following traits to leave my family line: Hopelessness, leave. Fear, leave. Confusion, leave. Powerlessness, leave. Anger, leave. Self-Devaluation, leave. Poverty, leave. Incarceration, leave. Unemployment, leave. Unfair wages, leave. Disintegration of Family, leave. Infidelity, leave. Abuse, leave.
(List any negative traits you feel your family still carry from slavery and tell it to leave).

Lord, please allow me, as a representative of my family line, to re-enter, through Christ's Door of entry, through the Power of the Holy Spirit, in Jesus' name.

I now stand before You Lord (actually stand, if you're able).
I declare as a representative of my entire family line, by the blood of the Lamb, I choose to walk (step forward, or put your hands in front of you like you're entering through a new door) through Your portal of life, liberty, and love, in the name of the Father, and the Son, and the Holy Spirit. Amen.

I bring through this new portal all that I know, all that my ancestors never had access to, and a future, designed by God, the Creator of this world.

Lord, please accept my re-entry into this nation, chain-free, mind-free, full of hope, full of anticipation for what You have in store for us!

Please Lord, restore all that was taken from our family. Make all things new for us.

Thank You Lord Jesus. We give You the glory and the honor and the praise.
In Jesus' name. Amen.

David Eltis and David Richardson, *Atlas of the Transatlantic Slave Trade*
Riverhttp://research.history.org/Historical_Research/Research_Themes/ThemeEnslave/SlaveTrade.cfm
Charleston's Walking Slave Tour – Fall 2012

2. BEING STOLEN

Father God, in the name of Jesus Christ, I ask that You would please break the curse of my family being stolen from their native land.

By the blood of the Holy Lamb of God, Jesus Christ, I cut, break, and sever all ties from the curse of being stolen from our native land, off my family line.

I cancel the curse to the ties of all those in my generational line that were
kidnapped,
snatched,
stolen,
dragged,
captured,
handcuffed,
bound,
gagged,
raped,
chained,
whipped into submission,
tied,
restrained,
bound by their feet, legs, waist, hands, arms, head, or neck,
muzzled,
blindfolded,
confused,
horrified,
terrorized,
stripped naked,
tortured,
betrayed,
bruised,
brutalized,
given over by enemies,
given over by friends,
given over by community leaders,
given over by neighbors,
or given over by acquaintances due to:
money, trade, lust, power, social climbing, blackmail, indifferences, religious discrepancies, religious differences, political gain, monetary gain; tribal, village, or nation competition or conflict; hatred, jealousies, loyalty to foreigners, loyalty to cultures, family obligations and commitments; betting; foolish (spur of the moment/last minute/rash) vows, foolish oaths, capital gains, misinterpretations of the Holy Scriptures, inhumanity, justification of inhumanity, superiority, laziness, non-accountability, bribes, love of cruelty, revenge, apathy, the need for developing

the infrastructure of the new colonies, the need of free labor to build them, the need for economic growth,
the development of the middle class, the drive for personal wealth and superiority, and the drive of global greed.

I cancel the curse of all forms of greed, that were responsible for the perpetuation of humiliation, dehumanization, and disassociation of members in my family line, that were stolen from the continents of Africa, Asia, Europe, North and South America, Australia, and any other parts of the world.

I cancel all ties to the curse of those in my family line that were captured against their wills, put into captivity, and sold or given away to serve in slavery or indentured servitude.

I break, break, break, break (say the word, "break", as many times as you feel necessary to break the chains of slavery off your family line) every chain that has enslaved the people of my family line.

Lord, I choose to forgive all those that were involved in the enslavement of my ancestors.

I choose to forgive all European and American businessmen, investors, bankers, brokers, lenders, managers, builders, merchants, entrepreneurs, nautical slave industries (including ships, crews, yards), all companies, businesses and firms that invested, traded, or profited from slavery and I choose to forgive their CEOs, boards, staff and shareholders.

I forgive all those whose buildings and roads were built on the backs of the free labor of my ancestors including all merchants, companies, businesses, firms, cities, towns, plantations, libraries, schools, households, churches, and government structures, roads and highways.

I forgive all Europeans, Africans, and Native Americans that were hired or used against their wills, to scout and capture my family members. I forgive them for their participation in the kidnapping of my African family members, who were stolen from their families, culture, and homeland, in order to become slaves in this foreign land.

I forgive everyone involved in the exploitation of my ancestors, including the descendants of any proprietors, businesses, societies, religious organizations, governments, buildings, trust funds, and manufacturers that also exist today.

I forgive all societies in America, North, South and Central, the Caribbean, Europe, Asia, including the Middle East, Africa including Egypt, Australia, the Pan Pacific Islands, including Laos, Samoa, Hawaii and all other nations where my ancestors were enslaved, OR where my ancestors participated in enslaving others. Please forgive all those in my family line that abused and enslaved people, in Jesus' name.

I forgive them all Lord Jesus, in Your name, and I ask that You would please forgive all those that I have listed, that participated in stealing people's lives.

I ask that You would break the curse of Slavery OFF MY FAMILY LINE, FOREVER, starting back to when the first people in my family line were enslaved, to me, to my children, and to my children's children, for a thousand generations

I break all chains of enslavement off me and my family line.
I stand in the gap of my generational line and break the chains
off our minds, off our hearts, off our souls, off our bodies, off our wills,
and I CHOOSE TO forgive all events concerning the abduction of everyone in my family line, by the Blood of the Lamb of Jesus Christ.

I forgive the terror my ancestors endured while being kidnapped.
I forgive the grueling ship crossing, lying in feces, the smell of death, the humiliation of being locked in chains.
I forgive and release the depression of being incarcerated in the holding cells both in Africa and America.
I forgive any other imagery that comes to mind that my ancestors possibly endured, in the name of Jesus.

Lord, please wash clean all the hurt, the pain, the injustice, the death, the shame, the humiliation, the alienation, the depression, the mental disconnect, the daily subjection to abuse, the torture, the segregation, the raping, the apathy, all damage that established itself in my family line, I bind in the name of Jesus, and I command it to leave, in the name of Jesus.

I ask Lord that You would seal all spiritual doors and windows, all spiritual floors and ceiling, and put a spiritual hedge of protection around my family, protecting what You have now done, by Your blood.

Now Lord, I ask that You would restore EVERYTHING that was stolen from me and my family line since my families' abduction, in Jesus' name.

Please restore Your spiritual wholeness, and faith.
Please grant us restitution, reparations and credit for all the free labor my family members performed, some, paying with their lives.

I ask this blessing of restoration for me, my children, my children's children, for a thousand generations, In the name of the One, Jesus Christ, Who makes all things possible, yesterday, today and forever. Amen.

DVD: *Slavery and the Making of America,* Director Dante J. James, Director Gail Pellett, Director Chana Gazit, and Director Leslie D. Farrell

3. BEING SOLD

Father, in the name of Jesus, I ask You to please break the curse of being sold as a commodity, off my family line.

I choose to forgive the selling of my family members. I choose to forgive all persons involved in the capturing, shipping, and purchasing of my ancestors, in markets thousands of miles away from their native homes.

I choose to forgive all people who benefitted from the selling of my family members, not caring about the psychological damage it placed on our family line. In the name of Jesus, as a representative of this family line, I break off ties to the following:
Anxiety, leave in the name of Jesus.
Nakedness, leave in the name of Jesus.
Hopelessness, leave in the name of Jesus.
Powerlessness, leave in the name of Jesus.
Shame, leave in the name of Jesus.
Claustrophobia, leave in the name of Jesus.
Anger, leave in the name of Jesus.
Despair, leave in the name of Jesus.
Confusion, leave in the name of Jesus.
Humiliation, leave in the name of Jesus.
Permanent separation from our native families abroad, leave in the name of Jesus.
All judgment against my family line based on our prowess, leave.
All judgment against my family line based on our intelligence, leave.
All judgment against my family line based on our monetary value, leave.
All forced separation of slave family members sold by owners or banks for profit, debt, or retribution when they misbehaved, leave in the name of Jesus.

I cut, break, and sever all ties to the curse of the selling of my ancestors. I cut and cancel any monetary value set on my ancestors. I cut off all ties to face value (appearance). I cut off and sever all monetary ties that were based on my ancestors' physicality, sexuality, stamina, talent, skill, loyalty and productivity. I cut off, bind and burn all legal and illegal purchasing transactions of my ancestors. By the blood of the Lamb, we are no longer property to ANYONE, any more. Our value is priceless in the eyes of the Lord.

I declare in the name of Jesus, we are FREE from monetary value, and I cancel all slavery off my family line, from every generation to the present, to me, to my children, and to my children's children, to a thousand generations.

I cancel all slavery and bondage off my family line from: any person, job, organization, society, secret society, town, country, political system, world system, business, bad friend(s), bad relationship(s), bad partnership(s), abusive family members, family obligations, credit cards, debt, incarcerations, illegal activities,

illegal organizations, illegal systems, religious cults, the occult, addictions, psychological baggage, idols, bad behavior, bad habits, misconceptions, gossip, too much drama, and from anything else that doesn't please the Living God.
In the name of Jesus of Nazareth, by the Blood He shed on the cross, and by the power of His resurrection, I choose to forgive and release all anger toward my ancestors' former captors, masters, and foremen.

I choose to forgive the entire industry that created and sustained slavery.
I choose to forgive all lawmakers, laws and governing bodies that upheld slavery.
I choose to forgive the hundreds of years my family members were enslaved.
I choose to forgive all monetary values assigned to my family members.
And if I hold any anger toward You Lord, for allowing this to happen to my family line, I choose to forgive You Lord, and I ask that You would forgive me for being angry at You, in Jesus' name.

I cut and break off all ties to the curse of post-slavery employment ideology, off me and my family line, Lord. I break every resistance made against me and my current family members to receive fair and proper compensation for the work we do. I break and expose every hidden agenda of our employers (racism, classism, favoritism, nepotism, etc.),that keep us from receiving the wages, salaries, promotions, and advancements we deserve, in the name of Jesus.

Although my family members were sold for a monetary price and worked for free, there was nothing free about their experience. I acknowledge they paid a heavy price in being slaves, Lord. So, in the name of Jesus, I ask Lord that You would restore all that was robbed from my family line.

I claim my Godly heritage, made possible by the Lord Jesus Christ, and I stand in my family line and claim for every slave in my family, their Godly heritage, ordained by God from the beginning of creation.

Please Lord, restore our family's joy, where we were once anxious.
Please Lord, restore our family's solidarity, where we were once sold off and separated.
Please Lord, restore our family's fidelity, where we were once forced to procreate with the masters for their pleasure, or to produce laborers for their productivity.
Please Lord cancel the curse of our children being looked at as a commodity (especially by drug-dealers), instead of children of the Living God.
Please restore recreation for our youth, so they may play freely.
Please restore all the moneys for the back breaking manual labor our family members performed, without being paid.

We want all that money back, Lord.
Please Lord, restore our health Lord; mind, body, and spirit to be in line with You Lord.
In the Name of the Father, Yahweh, the Son, Jesus, and the Holy Spirit. Amen

4. BEING BOUGHT

Father, in the name of Jesus, I ask that You would please break the curse of being bought, off my family line. I ask Lord that You would please forgive all transgressors of this sin.

Lord, in the name of Jesus, Son of the Living God, I cut, break, and sever every tie attached to the people in my family line that were purchased. On behalf of my family members, I cut, break, and sever all ties with all owners of my family. Whether legal or illegal, I nullify all contracts, deeds, or written bills of sales of my family members. I burn all documentation receipting their ownership, in the name of Jesus. As a member of this family line, I void all purchasing transactions of my ancestors, and I choose to forgive the humiliation that came from them being bought like chattel.

In the name of Jesus, I renounce all oaths or promises of dedications to servitude, sworn by my ancestors, to any master, family, plantation, business, establishment, town, city, state, nation, code, law, job, military or other persons, that were pledged against their wills, or freely given with their wills.

Lord, I confess, I have only one Master, and that is my Lord and Savior Jesus Christ, who has bought my freedom with His Blood on the Cross. I plead the Blood of Jesus over all binding contracts, bills of sale, congressional, state, and local laws pertaining to the discrepancies of my race. Lord, I ask that You cancel every single written documentation that granted, issued or ordained that my family members were legal property to be purchased, and not deemed worthy to be considered equal citizens of this nation.

In the name of Jesus, I remove all shackles, off our feet, hands, neck, back, legs, arms, and mind. I remove all whips, ropes, chains that bound my family members to stay in line. I cut, break and sever all physical, emotional, psychological ties, and blackmail ties that were used to keep my family members in tow. I cut, break, sever and burn all oaths, vows, and promises of freedom that were made and not kept by others. I cancel any oaths made by my family members (on the white side) that weren't kept. I choose to forgive all broken promises of freedom and release those that made them, in Jesus' name.

Lord, I stand in the gap of my ancestors who were bought. In the name of Jesus, I choose to forgive all people who purchased my family members. In the name of Jesus, I cut, cancel and break off all ties to the following:
Hate, leave.
Unforgiveness, leave.
Confusion, leave.
Shame, leave.
Need to escape or run-away spirit, leave.
Lack of control, leave.

Separation, leave.
Spiritual walls and barriers, leave.
Hopelessness, leave.
Oppression, leave.
Discouragement, leave.
Low self-value, leave.
Self-hatred, leave.
Self-affliction, leave.
Feeling trapped, leave.
Feeling guilty, leave.
Feeling lost, leave.
Feeling sad, leave.
Feeling like killing somebody, leave.
Criminal intent, leave.
Uncontrollable anger, leave.
Hatred of authority, leave.
All connections of trying to please the master, leave in the name of Jesus.
All connections to the fear of being sold from the plantation, leave in the name of Jesus.
All feelings of the inability to do the right thing today, leave in the name of Jesus.
All shut-down spirits that formed out of my slave family's helplessness, leave in the name of Jesus.
The inability to love, leave.
The inability to feel, leave.
The inability to grieve, leave.
The inability to care, leave.
The inability to be vulnerable, leave.
All psychoses (mental illness) that developed in my family due to slavery, leave in the name of Jesus.
All emotional scars that were carried by my family, due to witnessing and experiencing the cruelty of slavery, leave in the name of Jesus.
Powerlessness, leave.
Senselessness, leave.
Madness, leave.
Revenge, leave.
Hopelessness in God, leave.
Hopelessness in our future, leave.
Hopelessness in our communities, leave.
Betrayal, leave.
Doubt, leave.
Anger, leave.
Adultery, leave.
Philandering, leave.
Gambling, leave.
Drunkenness, leave.
Addiction, leave.

Abuse, leave.
The inability to commit, leave.
Self mutilation, leave.
Self torture, leave.
Suicide, leave.
Self-hatred , leave.
All hatred, leave in Jesus' name.

All nurturing emotions that were stymied, due to my ancestors' inability to fully protect their loved ones, during slavery and afterwards, return in the name of JESUS!

By the blood of the Lamb, I am free. By the blood of the Lamb, in the name of Jesus, I break the curse of slavery off every one in my family line, from the first slave in our family, to me, to my children, and to my children's children, for a thousand generations!

Thank you Father, for the privilege of standing in my family line and by Your Blood Lord Jesus, I release everyone in my family line, with the freedom given by Jesus Christ.

Lord please restore all joy back to my family line. All encouragement. All strength. All hope that was taken away. In the name of Jesus, please restore confidence, preservation of the family, incentive to work, to build, to dream, and to play.

I ask Lord that You would forgive all those on the white side of my family line that bought slaves and used slaves. I choose to forgive them, as well. All self-hatred, leave in the name of Jesus. Self-contempt, leave. Demoralization, leave. Lying, leave. Narcissism, leave. Entitlement, leave. Stealing, leave. Apathy, leave. Humiliating others, leave. Degrading others, leave. Dehumanizing others, leave. Devaluing other humans, leave. Lawlessness, leave. Obstructing God's law, leave. Reconstructing God's law for self-purposes, leave. Rape, leave. Adultery, leave,. Cruel intent, leave. Superiority, leave. Ranking, leave. Mental illness, leave. Hopelessness, leave. Health imbalance, leave. Doubt, leave. Blaming others, leave, Anger, leave. Violence, leave. Greed, leave. Lying, leave. False modesty, leave. Inability to keep promises, leave. Inability to keep commitments, leave. Inability to make decisions, leave. Inability to admit the obvious, leave. Inability to identify with the suffering, leave. Bigotry, leave. Classism, leave. Poverty leave. Shame leave. Scapegoating, leave,. Hatred, leave in the name of Jesus.

Lord please restore on the white side of my family line, reconciliation. Please restore peace, kindness, compassion, truth, and love, in the name of Jesus.

May the white and black blood ties, in my family line be reconciled in me, in my children, and in my children's children for a thousand generations, in the name of the Father, the Son and the Holy Spirit. Amen.

5. THE BAD THAT WAS BROUGHT OVER FROM AFRICA

Lord God, in the name of Jesus, by the Blood of the Lamb, I ask Lord, that You would remove from every part of my family line, all negative attributes that came over from our native continent of Africa, that were not pleasing to You.

I pray Lord, in the name of Jesus, that I cut, break, and sever all ties to witchcraft. Please forgive every person in my family line that participated in all practices of witchcraft, idolatry, voodoo, spiritual incantations, hexes, poisons, shaman potions, ungodly head priests' or priestess' blessings, sanctions of all satanic prayers, mysticism, worship of animals and objects, putting anything above, equal or below the power of God Almighty, the worship of all gods, pagan, local, or national, the practice of ungodly acts to gain power over someone, something, or some circumstance. All witchcraft, leave in the name of Jesus. Please cover me and all those in my family line with the blood of the Lamb.

Lord I stand in the gap of my family line and I humbly repent for all those in my family line that participated in these acts that weren't pleasing to You. I ask that You'd forgive us. Please remove all curses relating to all witchcraft practices, and please grant a hedge of protection around my family line, starting with me, my children and my children's children, to a thousand generations.

Lord, I stand in the gap of my family line, and I ask that You would remove all curses from our line, in which my family members were involved with sexual misconduct, adultery, multiple partners, multiple spouses, the using of men, women, or children as sexual objects, the selling of humans for sexual pleasure, any harmful or murderous acts pertaining to sex, the use of sex for status advancement, sex as a control, sex as a weapon, sex to befriend, sex against an enemy, or sex for jealousy.

Lord, I cut, break and sever all ties of jealousy and envy off my family line. Anyone in my family line that participated in jealousy that brought harm to others, I ask that You'd forgive them, Lord. I too forgive all those in my family line that participated in harmful acts caused by jealousy and envy. I renounce their acts and I apologize for any act that may have incurred Your wrath. I ask Lord, that You'd please remove the curse of jealousy and envy off my family line, and restore peace to my family, in Jesus' name.

In the name of Jesus, I break off all religious, cultural, tribal and national philosophies of superiority. I cancel all racial divisions between Arabs and Africans. I break off all European favoritism. I sever all inferiority and superiority ideologies amongst African peoples. I ask You Lord to please cancel such rankings. I choose to forgive all family members that participated in these acts. I repent for their actions, and apologize on their behalf, Lord.

I cancel, break, and cut all ties to the East Africa (Swahili/Arab/Indian/Persian) slave trade that sold slaves up and down the east coast, to the Middle East, and all over the world. I ask You Lord to please forgive these acts, and anyone in my family line that participated in them. I choose to forgive my family members that participated in these acts. I repent on their behalf, and I apologize, Lord.

I break off the curse of all public beatings, exposures of women's nakedness, all whipping and bullying as tests to show how strong African slaves were before purchasing, and the killing of those who proved to be of no value.

I cancel all in-house grudges, retaliations, and vindictiveness against countrymen after the British, French, Germans, and Portuguese abandoned the occupation of African nations.

I cut, break, and cancel all ties of embarrassment by light-skin blacks, of being called African in certain regions of Africa, because of the association of their forefathers being African slaves.

I cancel the curse of exploitation of Africa, stealing its land, stealing its resources, and devaluating its native population, for profit, gain and power. I stand in my generational line and I choose to forgive the abduction and trading of nearly 11 million Africans for the New World. I renounce the African kingdoms that were built and thrived off the betrayal of selling their own. I forgive the brutality of the slave traders. I forgive the black on black slave traders.

I break off the curse of the first European slave trading post of ELMINA, Ghana, to the last European slave trading post of OUIDAH, Benin, and the enslaving kingdoms of the Ashanti of KUMASI, Ghana and ABOMEY, Benin and ask Lord that You would cleanse these places and all places where we were betrayed by our own brethren. I choose to forgive them, and I ask that You would restore those places with the Blood of the Lamb.

In the name of Jesus, I cancel, break, and cut all ties to the places in Africa, marked as the rooms of no return, the doors of no return, and the gates of no return, that my ancestors experienced. I cancel all slave roads my ancestors had to journey, bound by chains, leaving their homeland to board slave ships.

By the Blood of the Lamb, I cancel, break, and unlock all doors of the inhumane and overcrowded detentions in all slave camps, prisons, castles, dungeons, holding posts, markets and cells, for months at a time in darkness, in African harbors. I release those in my family line from the curse of being held against their wills, waiting to be sold, in European slave buildings. I forgive all those who were involved, and I release everyone in my family line who were held in bondage there.

In the name of Jesus, I cut, break, and sever all ties to the diseases (malaria and yellow fever) that occurred, due to the overcrowded and inhumane conditions of the detention centers. I forgive the terror of death my ancestors witnessed, before even leaving Africa.

All thoughts of suicide as an only means of escape, leave in the name of Jesus!
All confusion of not knowing where they were going and
All fear of not knowing what was going to happen, leave in the name of Jesus!
All horror that was experienced on the slave ships, leave in the name of Jesus!
All complacency that developed, when forced to obey their captors, leave!
All feelings that "I have no control over my own life", leave in the name of Jesus!
Powerlessness, leave. Hopelessness, leave. Despair, leave. Fear, leave in the name of Jesus. The inability to fight, leave. Giving up, leave in the name of Jesus! Defiance met with torture, leave in the name of Jesus. Darkness, leave in the name of Jesus.

The ability to reason, return in the name of Jesus.
Sanity, return in the name of Jesus.
Bearings (where I'm from and where I'm going), return in the name of Jesus.

I renounce the curse of being used by Europeans to do their dirty work.
I renounce the curse of being used by Africans to do their dirty work.
I forgive all Africans and Europeans that participated in the raiding and selling of my ancestors. I cut and destroy all strings of being used as a puppet for someone else's personal gain, in the name of Jesus. I forgive all those who profited, from these acts.

I forgive all establishments of slavery, including the African slave systems that presided before the Europeans ever arrived in Africa. I forgive all Africans that enslaved my ancestors. I cancel all treaties and business negotiations with all African royalty, chieftains and political officials that partnered with the Europeans to sell and trade my ancestors.

I humbly ask Lord that You would forgive anyone in my family that participated in slave trading, willingly or unwillingly. I ask Lord that You would restore the relationships, resources, cultures, and inventions that were lost by slave trading. I ask Lord that You would destroy all caste systems that were established by Africans, before my family ever arrived in America. I break all caste system beliefs off my family line, in the name of Jesus, Who sees all men and women as equal. I specifically forgive the Ashantis, the Swahilis, and the Kings of Abomeyg, for making profits by participating in the slave trade.

I renounce the cultivating of superiority by warriors. I cut, break, and cancel all human blood sacrifices and body sacrifices, in walls of buildings, temples, and homes of conquerors. I break off any ties to family members who used human skulls as trophies.

I ask You Lord to please remove the generational guilt, from all my African ancestors who could not help their captured loved ones. Please cancel all feelings of survivor's guilt, grief, and abandonment off my family line in both the United States and Africa.

I break off all corruption, in the name of Jesus,
I break off all grudges, in the name of Jesus.
I cancel, break, and cut all ties to the curse of colonization, in the name of Jesus.
I break off all exploitation of natural resources, in the name of Jesus.
I break off all exploitation of people in low wages, for intense and dangerous work.
I break off the curse of Africans being the poorest people in the world.
I break off the curse of Africans having a third world classification.
I break off the curse of African slavery, U.S. slavery, and all global slavery.
I break off all global bigotry and misinformation by scholars and scientists who refused to believe Africans were capable of creating magnificent kingdoms.
I break off all the re-naming of African countries.
I break off all distortions and lies of Africa's past.
I cancel all unnecessary begging and bartering, in the name of Jesus.
I cancel the devaluation of Africa's history.
I cancel Europe and America's reclassification of who is African and who is Arab.
I break, cancel and cut off all practices of deity ceremonies, that are not of YOU.
I break, cancel and cut off all ties to the worship of ancestors (mythical or real).
I break, cancel and cut off all blood, human, animal, food, and earthly sacrifices.

Lord I cut, break and sever all ties to tribal gang war activity. Please forgive all those in my family line that have participated in tribal wars. While I am fully aware that in various times and places, tribal wars were culturally understandable, and necessary as a means of survival, I stand in the place of my family, and I humbly ask Lord that You would break off any ties to past and present tribal gangs that assembled to Your displeasure. Please forgive my family members who brought shame by participating. I ask You to please cancel all allegiances to any tribe, war lord, gang, crew, or gathering that are NOT of You. Please cancel all ties to tribal gang mentality that are NOT of You. Please bring peace to my family line, Lord, in the name of Jesus, by the blood of the Lamb. Please protect all my family members, currently from all tribal gang activity, and we ask that You Lord would please disband the spirit of negative tribal gangs in our land, in the name of Jesus, so that all people in this country can live in peace.

Lord, I ask that You would cut, break and sever all ties to anyone European in my family line, that participated in the persecution of Africans. Lord I'm sorry for all those in my family that caught, sold, enslaved, beat, killed, humiliated, or destroyed African families, tribes, cultures, towns, cities, societies, governments, nations, or African kingdoms.

That's a lot of sin God. I ask for the forgiveness of those family members, and I ask that You would lift the curse of their actions off our family line. Please restore our family line to Your glory, in Jesus' name. Amen

DVD: *Wonders of the African World with Henry Louis Gates Jr.,* Director Nicola Colton, Director Nick Godwin, and Director Helena Appio
http://sacredsites.com/africa/mali/dogon.html

6. WORSHIPING DEITIES FROM AFRICA

Lord God, please break the curse of worshiping false gods off my family line, in the name of Jesus Christ of Nazareth.

Lord Jesus, please forgive all my African ancestors (and ancestors from every Continent) for worshiping anyone or anything that wasn't You, the true and living God. I'm so sorry Lord, for all those in my family line that participated in bowing down to anything or anyone other than You. Please accept my humble apology, and please break off the curse that was placed on our line, due to their idolatry. I repent for their actions, and I choose to forgive all family members that brought this curse on our family, by practicing idolatry. Please cleanse us from idolatry, and restore our faith in You.

In the name of Jesus Christ of Nazareth, I cut, break and sever all ties to the curse of idolatry from my family line.

Lord I cut, break, and sever all ties to territorial spirits that were summoned by my family members. I am VERY sorry for any family member of mine that participated in such a foolish act. Please forgive all family members that participated and still participate in such practices. I ask Lord that You would correct this atrocity immediately and send all territorial spirits to the place You, Lord Jesus, would have them to go.

In the Name of JESUS, I command all spirits that my family members engaged in, to be removed from my family line, by the Blood of the Lamb, JESUS CHRIST OF NAZARETH. ANY and ALL spirits must leave now. I break, cut, and sever all ties to all spirits, deities, and false gods:

I break, cut and sever all ties to the following:

A
Abassi – Nigerian creator god and lord of the sky
Abiku
Abuk
Achimi
Adriambahomanana
Adro
Adroa
Adroanzi
Age
Aha Njoku
Aho Njoku
Aigamuxa
Ajok

Akongo
Ala
Ale
Alla
Alouroua
Amma
Ananse
Anansi
Andriamahilala
Andriambahomanani
Andumbulu
Ane
Anotchi
Asa
Atai
Ataokoloinona
Aunt Nancy
Awa – practices ()
Azra'il
Azrail

B
Ba Dimo
Babalu Aye
Babaluaye
Babayanmi
Badimo
Banga
Bayani
Bayanni
Binu – practices
Bomazi
Buk
Buku
Bumba

C
Cagn
Candit
Cghene
Chango
Chedi Bumba
Chiuta
Chonganda
Chuku

D
Da
Deng
Ditaolane
Domfe
Dongo
Dubiaku
Dxui
Dyinyinga
Dziva,

E
Ebore
Edinkira
Egungun Oya
Ekurana
Elegua
En Kai
Enekpe
Engai
Enkai
Eseasar
Eshu
Esu
Evus

F
Fa
Faro

G
Ga Gorib
Gamab
Gaunab
Ghekre
Gu
Gunab

H
Haitse Aibeb
Haitsi Aibeb
Haiuri
Hare
Heitsi

Heitsi Eibib
Huntin
Huveane
Hyel
Hyel Taku
I
Iamanjie
Imana
Itherther
Iyakare
J
Jakuta
Jok
Jok Odudu
Juok
K
Kaang
Kabundungulu
Kaka Guie
Kalumba
Kammapa
Kamonou
Kamunu
Kanu
Katonda
Khakhabaisaywa
Khodumodurno
Khonvoum
Khuzwane
Kintu
Kumunu
Kwoth
L
Le Eyo
Legba
Lebe – the earth god Lela
Leza
Libanza
Lisa
M
Maori
Massassi
Massim Biambe
Mawu

Mawu Lisa
Mbaba Mwanna Waresa
Mbere,
Mbokomu
Mbombo
Mbongo
Mboya
Mebege
Mebeghe
Mebere
Minga Bengale
Minona
Mo Dimo
Mobokomu
Modimo
Morimi
Morongo,
Moshanyana
Mugai
Mukunga M'bura
Mukunga Mbura
Mukuru
Muluku
Mulungu
Musso Koroni
Mwambu
Mwambwa
Mwari
Mwuetsi

N
Naiteru Kop
Nana Buluku
Nasilele
Natero Kop
Naz
Ndjambi
Ndrian
Ndriananahary
Ndriananhary
Neiterkob
Neiternkob
Neiterogob
Ngai

Ngewo Wa
Nialith
Nimba
Ninepone
Ninepone Mebeghe
Njambe
Njambi
Njambi Karunga
Njemakati
Nkwa
Nommo
None
None Mebeghe
Nummo
Nyaliep
Nyalitch
Nyambe
Nyambe(2)
Nyame
Nyaminyami
Nyankopon
Nyikang
Nyiko
Nyingone Mebeghe
Nyokonan
Nyonye Ngana
Nzambi
Nzame
Nzame Mebeghe

O
Obambo
Obambou
Obassi Osaw
Obatala
Ochosi
Odomankomo
Odua
Ododu
Odudua
Oduduwa
Ofo
Oghene
Ogo

Ogun
Olodumare
Olokun
Olorun
Olufon
Olurun
Omukuru
Omumborombanga
Omumborombonga
Onyame
Onyankopon
Orisa
Orisala
Orishala,
Orishas
Orixa
Oromila
Orula
Orunmila
Osanyin
Oshe
Oshun
Oshunmare
Osun
Oya,

P
Pale Fox
Pemba

Q
Qamata
Qamta
Quamta

R
Rada
Raluvumbha
Rugaba
Rugira
Ruhanga
Rurema
Ruwa

S
Sagbata
Sakarabru
Sakpata
Shadipinyi
Shakpana
Shango
She
Soko
Somtup
Sopona
Sudika Mbambi

T
Thixo
Tilo
Tore
Tsetse Bumba
Tsui
Tsui //goab
Tsui Goab

U
Uhlanga
Umvelinqangi
Unkul
Unkulunkulu
Uthlanga

W
Waaqa
Waaqa Tokkichaa
Wak
Waq
Wele
Were
Woyengi
Wulbari
Wuni
Wuona
Wuonji
Wuonkwere
Wuonoru

X
Xango,
Y
Yansan
Yasigi
Yeban
Yemanja
Yemaya
Yemayah
Yemonja
Yurugu,
Z
Zanahary

I renounce and repent for all worshiping and sacrificing to these names, and any other names I missed, in the name of Jesus.

Please Lord, cleanse all areas where these spirits have been permitted to roam. Please put a spiritual hedge of protection around our families, by the Blood of the Lamb, Lord Jesus. Please Lord, lift any curses that were established by these practices and restore, gracious Father, anything the enemy was allowed to steal, kill or destroy. Please protect us from re-entering any of these practices, in Jesus' name. Please restore complete spiritual dependency on You, in our family line, Lord, to me, to my children, and to my children's children, to a thousand generations. Amen

Lord, I ask for peace to those who do not acknowledge You and I ask that I would be a living example of Your Love, in Jesus' name. Amen

http://sacredsites.com/africa/mali/dogon.html
http://www.godchecker.com/pantheon/african-mythology.php?deity=

Lord, I humbly ask that You please remove the curse of worshiping specific Egyptian gods off my family line, in the name of Jesus. Lord, please forgive all family members that participated in this act. I repent for their actions, and I choose to forgive them, as well.

In the Name of JESUS CHRIST OF NAZARETH, I break, cut, and sever all ties to the curse of worshipping all Egyptian gods off my family line. By the Blood of the Lamb, I command ALL Egyptian spirits to leave now, in the name of Jesus.

I break, cut and sever all ties to the following Egyptian gods:

A

Aa
Aah
Aapep
Abtu
Ah
Ahemait
Ahti(2)
Ailuros
Aken
Aker
Amathaunta
Amaunet
Amemait
Amen
Amen Ra
Amen Re
Amenhotep
Ament
Amentet
Amentit
Ammam
Ammit
Ammon
Ammon Ra
Ammon Re
Ammut
Amn
Amon
Amon Ra
Amon Re
Amsit

Amun
Amun Ra
Amun Re
Anat
Andjety
Anedjti
Anet
Anezti
Anhur
Anit
Ankh
Ankhet
Ankt
Anouke
Anpu
Anti
Anubis
Anuket
Apademak
Apedemak
Apep
Apepi
Apet
Apis
Apophis
Aptet
Arensnuphis
Ari Hes Nefer
Arsnuphis
Aset
Aten
Aten Ra
Aten Re
Aton
Aton Ra
Aton Re
Atum
Atum Ra
Atum Re

B
Ba
Ba Neb Tetet
Ba Pef

Bab
Babay
Babi
Baneb Djedet
Banebdedet
Banebdjedet
Banebdjetet
Banebtetet
Banephthysdjedet
Bast
Bastet
Bat
Bata
Benu
Bes
Beset
Book of the Dead
Buto

C
Chenti Cheti
Chenti Irti
Chepri
Cherti
Chnemu
Chnoumis
Chnum
Chnuphis
Chons
Chontamenti
Cneph

D
Dedun
Dedwen
Dua
Duamutef

E
Ehi
Ernutet

G
Geb

H

Ha(2)
Haap
Hah
Hap
Hapi
Hapy
Har Nedj Hef
Har Pa Khered
Har Pa Khruti
Harensnuphis
Harmakhis
Harmatchis
Haroeris
Harpakhered
Harpakhruti
Hat Mehit
Hathor
Hatmehit
Hatmehyt
Hauhet
Hedetet
Heget
Heh
Hehet
Hek
Heket
Hektet
Hemen
Hemsut
Hemuset
Henet
Hep
Hepi
Heptet
Heqet
Heret
Herishep
Heru Behudti
Hesa
Hesat
Het Mehit
Hetmehit
Hez Ur

Hike
Horus
Hu
Huh

I

Iat
Ibis
Ienpw
Ihu
Ihy
Imentet
Imeut
Imhetep
Imhotep
Imiut
Imset
Imsety
Inher
Inmutef
Inpu
Ipet
Iptet
Ipy
Isis
Iunmutef

J

Joh

K

Ka
Kauket
Keb
Kebechet
Kebechsenef
Kehperi
Kek
Keket
Keku
Kemu
Kemur
Kemwer
Ken

Khem
Khensu
Kheper
Khepera
Khepri
Kherty
Khnemu
Khnum
Khons
Khonsu
Kneph
Knouphis
Kuk

L

Lenpw

M

Ma'at
Maat
Mafdet
Maftet
Mahes
Mehen
Mehet Uret
Mehet Weret
Mehturt
Mehurt
Menchit
Mendes
Menhit
Menthu
Mentu
Meret
Meretseger
Mert
Mertseger
Meskhenet
Meskhent
Min
Mnevis
Mnewer
Month
Monto
Mut

N

Naunet
Neb Hut
Nebthet
Ned Er Tcher
Nef
Nefer Tem
Nefer Temu
Nefertem
Nefertum
Nehab
Nehebkau
Nehebkhau
Nehebu Kau
Neit
Neith
Nekhabed
Nekhbet
Neper
Nephthys
Nepit
Neteraantmwmw
Nu
Nuit
Nun
Nunet
Nut

O

Ogdoad
Onuris
Opet
Osiris

P

Petbe
Ptah
Ptha

Q

Qadesh
Qadeshet
Qeb
Qetesh
Qudshu

R

Ra
Re
Renenet
Renenutet
Renpet
Reret
Reret Weret
Reshep
Reshpu

S

Sag
Sahu
Sakhmet
Sal
Satet
Seb
Sebek
Seker
Sekhet
Sekhmet
Selket
Selkit
Sep
Sepa
Septu
Serket
Serquet
Seshat
Sesmu
Set
Setekh
Setesh
Seth
Seti
Shai
Shait
Shay
Shed
Shenty
Shesmetet
Shu
Sobek

Sochet
Sokar
Sokaris
Soker
Sons of Horus
Sopd
Sopdet
Sopdu
Sopedu
Sothis
Sphinx
Su
Suchos
Sutekh

T

Tahuti
Tatenen
Taueret
Taurt
Taweret
Tefen
Tefenet
Tefnet
Tefnut
Tehuti
Tem
Temu
Thoeris
Thot
Thoth
Tphenis
Tum
Tutu

U

Uadjet
Ubastet
Un
Un Nefer
Uneg
Unut
Usire

W

Wadj Wer

Wadjet
Waset
Wenut
Wepawet
Wosret
Wosyet
Y
Yinepu

I renounce and repent for all worshipping and sacrificing to these names, and any other names I missed, in the name of Jesus.

Please restore to my family line, all the gifts and talents we inherited from You in Africa; of medicine, architecture, artistic design, politics, negotiation, economic development, art, intelligence, academics, culinary arts, fashion, scholars of the Holy Scriptures, science, entertainment, humor, love, family, culture, innovation, servant hood, respect, and joy, in Jesus' name. Amen!

http://www.godchecker.com/pantheon/egyptian-mythology.php?deity=

7. THE GOOD THAT WAS BROUGHT OVER FROM AFRICA

Father, in the name of Jesus, I ask that You would please bring back and restore, what You have given our people from the continent of Africa. Please fully restore the richness and beauty in us, which was robbed or diminished by colonization and slavery.

I choose to forgive those who took away these blessings from my family line, and I humbly ask Lord, that the following gifts and talents be restored to my family, in Jesus' name:

Good Kings and Kingdoms
Good Queens
Just Rulers
Cultivators of Transportation: land, sky, and sea
Architects
Agriculturists
Constructors
Project Managers
Skilled Laborers
Local, National and International Traders
Industrialists
Architects of Technology
All Complexions Tolerated and Celebrated
Artists
Interior Decorators
Builders of Societies
Architects of Civilizations
Educators
Historians
Negotiators
Authors
Conquerors
Linguists
Founders of Colleges and Universities
Horticulturalists
Irrigators
Travelers
Adaptors of Environments
Celebrators of Marriages
Defenders of Empires and Families
Joyful Celebrators
Physicians
Healers
Naturalists
Politicians

Orators
Developers
Founders of Institutions
Merchants
Sultans
Petitioners
Policy Writers
City Planners
Engineers
Designers of Indoor Plumbing
Designers of Cities and Kingdoms
Interracial Marriages
Identity Security

The Blessings of Ethiopia:
Creators of Christian Festivals
Executors of City-Wide Christian Celebrations
Thousands of Years of Christian Dynasties
Christian Empires
Christian Royalty
Master Builders
Designs of Holy Cities
Hewing Churches Out of Mountain Sides
Sanctity
Holiness

Creators of Great Libraries
Librarians
Dancers
Musicians
Poets
Founders of Universities Like the Great University of Timbuktu
Scholars
 Professors
Authors
Astronomers
Scientists
Masters of their domains
Wealthy
God fearing

We want it all back, Lord. For me, for my children, for my children's children, and for my family for a thousand generations. In Your Son Jesus' name, we pray. Amen.

DVD: *Wonders of the African World with Henry Louis Gates, Jr.*, Director Nicola Colton, Director Nick Godwin, and Director Helena Appio
Hazel Richardson, *Life in Ancient Africa*

8. DISHONORING GOD

Father, in the name of Jesus, please remove the curse of dishonoring You, off my family line. I humbly apologize for everyone in my family line that dishonored You. I stand in the gap of my family line and I ask that You would forgive us for anything and everything that we did, that was displeasing to You. As a representative of this family line, I repent for all their actions, Lord.

In the name of Jesus, I cut, break and sever all ties to the curse of dishonoring the living God. I choose to forgive all family members that incurred Your wrath, because of their actions.
In the name of Jesus, I command all the following to leave my family line:
All idols and idolatry, leave in the name of Jesus.
All worship of dolls and models of dolls, leave in the name of Jesus.
All demonic blood sacrifices, leave in the name of Jesus.
All human body and limb sacrifices of adults and children, leave in the name of Jesus.
All incantations, leave in the name of Jesus.
All accumulation of body parts, animal parts, and inanimate objects for sacrificing, leave. All evil deeds performed, (especially under orders of witch doctors or priests), leave.
All alliances, oaths and vows with evil, leave in the name of Jesus.
All sexual acts committed and tied to witchcraft, leave in the name of Jesus.
All amulets, break. All charms, break. All hexes, break.
All things given power from evil, to produce good luck, leave in the name of Jesus.
Séances leave. Transcendental-states, leave. Potions, leave. Bloodletting leave.
Satanic rituals, break off in the name of Jesus.
Demon possession, leave in the name of Jesus.
The practice of magic (white, black, or any other color), leave in the name of Jesus.
All spells and demonic prayers, leave by the Blood of Jesus Christ of Nazareth.
The giving of children for evil, leave in the name of Jesus.
The giving of women for evil, leave in the name of Jesus.
The giving of men for evil, leave in the name of Jesus.
The taking of people's freedom, leave in the name of Jesus.
The worshiping of nature and animals, leave in the name of Jesus.
All festivals to deities, leave. All traditions and holidays of deities, leave.
All food sacrifices to deities, leave. All soul ties to deities, leave.
All mocking of God (sorry God) leave, in the name of Jesus.
All blasphemy, leave in the name of Jesus.
All vulgar acts in Your Holy Places, leave in the name of Jesus.
All anger my family members had toward You, leave in the name of Jesus.
All acts of making ourselves deities, leave in the name of Jesus.

Sorry Lord for all this foolishness. Please forgive all those in my family line that participated in these offenses. Please restore our faith to only honor You.
In Jesus' name. Amen.

9. COLONIZATION

Lord, in the name of Jesus Christ, I ask that You would please break the curses of colonization off my family line, and off this nation.

In the name of Jesus, I cut, break, and sever all ties off my family line, to the curses of colonization that were formed in this country. I choose to forgive the Portuguese, the Spanish, the Dutch, Swedes and Finns, the British, the French, the Russians, the Mexicans, and the Catholic Church (and any other nation or institution) for bringing the curses of colonization on my family line and on this nation.

I ask Lord that You would please forgive all family members (particularly on my white side) and non-family members, who offended You with acts of entitlement and enslavement, killing or stealing whatever they wanted, pushing aside one group over another, and using Your name as an excuse to take what wasn't theirs. Please forgive my family members who blasphemed Your name, claiming it was Your will for them to take other people's land, possessions, or freedom.

I choose to forgive all family members and non-family members that participated in stealing land from Native Americans, killing any tribes or people that got in their way. I choose to forgive them stealing Africans, to work the land that they stole to build their homes and fortunes. I choose to forgive all family and non-family members who exploited, depleted, and polluted this land for capital gain.

I choose to forgive all family members and non-family members that contributed to the demoralization of people, taking away their humanity and dignity for their own self purposes. I forgive all objectifying of people, all guilting people through religion, and all social ranking done by family members and non-family members, in order to control others, while justifying their actions. All those in my family and outside my family, that said they were doing these things in Your name Lord, please forgive them. Please forgive us.

In the name of Jesus, I break off all entitlement. I break off all control. I break off all social ranking. I break off all dehumanization. I break off all objectifying. I break off all religious guilt. I break off all demoralization, in Jesus' name.

Shame, leave. Anger, leave. Hostility, leave. Piracy, leave. Exploitation, leave. Vengeance, leave. Self-doubt, leave. Ambiguity, leave. Guilt, leave. Blame, leave.

Not excluding all the atrocities of U.S. colonization, it's historically noted that five years into the Revolutionary war, the British overtook the South. The British instilled their common practice of placing one societal group, in command over another. In this case, "the loyalists", who were newly settled poor white immigrants, were put in command over the established rich white southern gentry, who were thought to be "the rebels". As with other nations the British did this too, there was already major animosity between the loyalists and the rebels.

In 1780, their animosity turned into the first American civil war between whites, in the south. There was major brutality that occurred on both sides. Even if white southerners were neutral, they were victims of brutality and death.

White people Lord, were killing white people, torturing them, pulling out babies from wombs, beheading, writing epitaphs in their victims' blood, stealing, burning down farms, all in the name of patriotism, because of the British. It became the poor vs. the rich. The established vs. the newcomers. The newly empowered vs. the old guard. Resentment turned into empowerment, which turned into revenge, which turned into barbarism. The British also promised slaves their freedom, only to use them as free laborers for their military camps, and then as human shields once the British saw they were losing the war.

Please forgive this time in American history Lord, and burn the root causes of its conflict. Please forgive all those who participated in these barbaric acts. Please break the curse of British placement of one societal group over another, and put an end to all the generational resentment that came out of it. Please bring harmony among all societal groups in America, in Jesus' name. If my family members were a part of the 1780 civil war, please forgive us, Lord. If we were victims of that period, I choose to forgive all those who were brutal to us.

All negative roots established by colonization in the U.S., leave in Jesus' name.
Entitlement, leave in the name of Jesus.
Superiority, leave in the name of Jesus.
Inferiority, leave in the name of Jesus.
Division, leave in the name of Jesus.
Resentment, leave in the name of Jesus.
Violence, leave in the name of Jesus.
Revenge, leave in the name of Jesus.
Anger, leave in the name of Jesus.
Rebellion, leave in the name of Jesus.
Spirit of lynching, leave in the name of Jesus.
Spirit of brutality, leave in the name of Jesus.
Mob mentality, leave in the name of Jesus.

Equality, return. Love for our neighbor, return. Kindness, return. Self-respect, return. Self-awareness, return. Self-esteem, return. Joy, return. Humanity, return. Self-control, return. Responsibility, return. Love, return. In Jesus' name, Amen.

Lord, please bring peace to the places where colonization cultivated chaos.
Please blend our country to exist as one nation.
Please cancel the great divide of our nation, so we may all live in peace, tolerance, and love, in the name of Jesus Christ of Nazareth. Amen.

DVD: *Liberty! The American Revolution,* Director Ellen Hovde and Director Muffie Meyer
DVD: *Slavery and the Making of America,* Director Dante J. James, Director Gail Pellett, Director Chana Gazit, and Director Leslie D. Farrell
http://en.wikipedia.org/wiki/Colonial_history_of_the_United_States

10. NATIONAL FEAR

Father, in the name of Jesus, I ask that You would please remove the national curse of fear off my family line, and off this nation.

Lord, I cut, break, and sever all ties to the national curse of fear off my family, and off our country.

I ask that You would please remove all fear that was established through the founders of this country and its elite.
I ask that You remove all established by-laws that categorized blacks as inferior.
I ask Lord that You would remove all foundations of fear, that were put into place to keep blacks inferior and subservient.

I ask Lord that You, heavenly Father, would take away the national fear that keeps people wary of our black presence,
wary of our black talents,
wary of our being able to share in the wealth of this nation,
wary of us living side by side,
wary of us worshiping side by side,
wary of us contributing to national civic planning,
wary of us contributing to national scholastic curriculum,
wary of us contributing to national judicial by-laws,
wary of us contributing to liberating national, state, and county prison policies,
wary of us contributing to employment solutions,
wary of us contributing to technology, theology, art, sciences, literature, medicines, sports (in ownership as well as participation), all aspects of the entertainment industry, all aspects of the fashion industry, architecture, the auto industry, housing developments, academia, public policies, philanthropy, military strategies and anything else in this nation that has been monopolized by the very few.

Lord, I apologize for all those in my family line that initiated and participated (white or black), in filtering fear into our national consciousness. I repent for their actions, and I ask that You would please forgive us.

I choose to forgive my ancestors for promoting the propaganda of fear, and I forgive my current family members and myself (if applies) for spreading the fear of blacks, whites, and other races.

I apologize every time I stereotyped people. I apologize every time I was in fear of people, without cause (list every time you said something that was fear based and repent to God).

I give You my fear Lord (list EVERYTHING that you're afraid of and give it to God).

Fear, leave in the name of Jesus.
Phobias, leave in the name of Jesus.
Immobilization, leave in the name of Jesus.
Past failures, leave in the name of Jesus.
Past bad relationships, leave in the name of Jesus.
Sadness, leave in the name of Jesus.
Judgments, leave in the name of Jesus.
Guilt, leave in the name of Jesus.
Hatred, leave in the name of Jesus.
Blame, leave in the name of Jesus.
Bad memories of our family's history, be forgiven in the name of Jesus.
Bad memories of our nation's history, be forgiven in the name of Jesus.
The burden of the past, leave in the name of Jesus.
The fear of progress, leave in the name of Jesus.
The fear of change, leave in the name of Jesus.
The fear of one another, leave, in the name of Jesus.

National love, come in Jesus' name.
National joy, return in Jesus' name.
National hope, return in Jesus' name.
National harmony, return in Jesus' name.
National kindness, return in Jesus' name.
Memories of God's goodness, return in Jesus' name.

Lord, I choose not to live in fear any more.
I give You ALL MY FEAR, in Jesus' name.

Please do a new thing in our lives.
Please help us not to be bound to repeat the history of our ancestors.

Lord, Your mercies are new every morning!
Great is Thy faithfulness!

I claim Your blessings from fear, in the name of Jesus.
For me, for my children, and for my children's children, for a thousand generations.

In Jesus' name. Amen.

11. A BAD PARTNER

Father, please, in the name of Jesus, remove the curse of bad partners off my family line.

Be it marriage partners, business partners, friendships partners, even family members, please disassociate me and my family line from all bad partnerships.

By the power invested in me, as a member of this family, I cut, sever, and break all ties to the curse of bad partners off my family line.

Lord, I choose to forgive the person in my family line that introduced this curse to our family. I repent for their actions, and ask for forgiveness for them. I don't know who they ripped off, but I apologize and repent for their actions. I ask that You would please restore all that was stolen from their victims.

Lord please forgive all those in my family line that have perpetuated this curse. I choose to forgive them as well.

I ask that You would please restore to our family line, that which the enemy has stolen and taken away.

Please Lord, grant us discernment when we're coming across a bad deal.

Please Lord, show us when we're coming across a bad partner(s), even if they are friends or family.

Please Lord, give us clear signs as to whether we should partner with a person(s) or their proposal, even if it looks good to everyone else.

Please Lord, grant us a lion's heart to say "no" or to turn that person(s) away.

Please Lord, take away that pride or emotion that blocks us from seeing the true character of a person and help us to see all the risks behind their proposal.

Please Lord, throw a spotlight on a potential bad partner's qualities, so we can clearly see that they aren't the right person to invest in.

And even when we fail to see the clues, please block all transactions (protecting our heart and assets) until we can fully understand that You are not for this partnership.

This is a hard thing Lord.

We want to have good partners.
We want to make money.
We want to have lasting relationships.

We want to make good business deals.

But sometimes we are driven by our greed, lust, neediness, or desperation, and we can't see straight. Or, even when we know it's a bad partner, we don't have enough faith to believe You can send us someone or something better.

So, I renounce the lie, that to have something bad, is better than having nothing at all.

I renounce the lie, that to have someone bad, is better than having no one at all.

I renounce all bad partnerships in my life and in my family's line, and I break all soul ties to all bad partners in the past.

I'm sorry when we lower our standards, Lord, when You want the very best for us.

I repent for every bad partner I had, whether on purpose, or by accident (list every bad partner you or your family members were with, forgiving them, then forgiving yourself).

Bad partners, leave.
Anger, leave.
Selfishness, leave.
Blame, leave.
Paralyzed in making good decisions, leave.
Self-doubt, leave.
Stubbornness, leave.
Hate, leave.
Mistrust, leave.

I ask You Lord, to please restore, all that the enemies of our souls, have stolen.

Please bring good partners into our lives.

Good partners, come.
Joy, return.
Love, return.
Trust, return.
Hope, return.
New ideas, return.
Prosperity, return.
Sharing, return.

Please grant me, my children, and my children's children, for a thousand generations, good partners that we can trust, for the rest of our lives.
In Jesus' name. Amen.

12. ABANDONMENT

Lord, there seems to be a curse over me, where everybody leaves me. This may not be a curse, but it feels like one, so I'm going to remove it, just in case.

So Lord, in the name of Jesus, I ask that You would please remove the curse of abandonment off me and my family line.

I stand before You Lord Jesus. By the power vested in me as a member of this family, I cut, sever, and break all ties to the curse of abandonment, in the name of Jesus, from my family line.

I ask You Lord to please forgive the family member that introduced this curse to our family. Please forgive every family member who has since, participated in abandoning their family, friends, or commitments. Please forgive every act of abandonment that was committed by our family line, from the past, to the present, including myself (if applies).

I choose to forgive the family member who brought this curse on my family line, and I forgive everyone in the family line who participated in it.

I choose to forgive all events of abandonment that happened in my own life (list every event where you felt abandoned). I forgive every person who participated in these events (list each person, even if they didn't mean to abandon you OR they didn't know they were abandoning you).

All feelings of abandonment, leave in the name of Jesus.
All negative emotions tied to the feelings of abandonment, leave.
Sadness, leave.
Depression, leave.
Loneliness, leave.
All feelings of being unloved, leave.
All feelings of being unwanted, leave.
All hurt, leave.
Lies leave.
All feelings of "not being enough for the other person", leave.
All feelings of not being pretty enough, leave.
All feelings of not being handsome enough, leave.
All feelings of not being rich enough, leave.
All feelings of not being smart enough, leave.
All feelings of not being talented enough, leave.
All feelings of not being tall enough or short enough, leave.
All feelings of not being thin enough, leave.
All feelings of not being young enough or old enough, leave.
All feelings of not being cool enough, leave in Jesus' name.

Anything that makes me feel like I'm the reason I don't fit in or belong, anywhere, LEAVE, in the name of Jesus!
Lack of confidence, leave.
Over confidence, leave.
Shame, leave.
Self-doubt, leave.
Destructive thoughts, leave.
The inability to focus, leave.
Chemical-dependence, leave.
Emotional dependence, leave.
Food addiction, leave.
Sexual addictions, leave.
Drug addictions, leave.
All addictions, leave.
Sleep deprivation, leave.
Complete dependency on media or technology, leave.
All co-dependencies, leave.
All fear, leave.
All inability to commit, leave.
Distrust, leave.
Anger, leave.
Violence, leave.
All lack of self-control, leave.
All lies that "nobody loves me" leave.
All pickiness, leave.
All self-righteousness, leave.
All judgments of others, leave.
Jealousy, leave.
Grudges, leave.
Gossip, leave.
Improper thoughts, leave.

I forgive all those that hurt me, by leaving me. I ask for Your power Lord, to no longer be emotionally attached to those who continually abandon me. Help me to forgive them, and to move on.

Lord, please replenish what the locust have taken away, granting me new relationships with people who wish to stay.
Love, return.
Self-esteem, return.
Self-purpose, return.
Joy, return.
Healthy relationships, return.
Love, return.
Peace within, return.
In Jesus' name. AMEN!

13. ABUSE

Father, in the name of Jesus, I ask that You would please remove the curse of abuse from our family line.

As a member of this family, I stand in the gap and cut, break, and sever all ties to the curse of abuse off our family line.

Lord, please forgive the family member that introduced this curse to our family line. Also please forgive every family member in our family's past, who was abusive to others (list each action and repent to God on their behalf).
I humbly apologize for their actions.

Lord, this may not be easy, but I choose to forgive all abusive actions by my immediate family members, in Jesus' name. (List the abuse by your immediate family, repent to God on their behalf, then you forgive them. Name every incident. This could take a while. Remember, you may not feel like forgiving them, but it's important to let it go, so you can receive spiritual healing, and move on.)

Lord, please forgive all those (people or systems) outside my family line that have been abusive to my family members, in Jesus' name. I choose to forgive them (list, repent to God on their behalf, then you forgive them).

Lord, please forgive all those (people or systems) outside my family line that have been abusive to me, in Jesus' name. I choose to forgive them (list those who have been abusive to you, ask God to forgive them, then you forgive them).

Here are some examples:
I choose to forgive the people who abusively kidnapped my family from Africa.
I choose to forgive the jailers who abusively held my family hostage in the holding cells before shipping my family off to America.
I choose to forgive the slave ship crews, companies and stockholders who abusively chained my family for long and inhumane voyages to America.
I choose to forgive all slave traders for the abusive way they handled my family line, once arriving, demoralizing them with their harsh methods of selling.
I choose to forgive the abusive system of slavery in this country for centuries.
I choose to forgive how my family was sold off, sometimes not together.
I choose to forgive the abusive way they were devalued, and cast as non-human.
I choose to forgive the abusive system of Jim Crow.
I choose to forgive the abusive way my family members were not allowed to learn the way we wanted, vote the way we wanted, live where we wanted, or get paid the way they wanted.
I choose to forgive the abuse suffered by racial inequality and prejudice.
I choose to forgive the abuse suffered, in the name of a joke or because of a grudge.
I choose to forgive myself and any other family member, for internalizing the abuse, and taking our frustrations out on others.

Lord, I'm sorry for any time I was abusive to others, especially the ones I love (list and forgive yourself every time you did this).
Please forgive me, and please make me aware when I am being abusive.

Abuse, leave in the name of Jesus.
Anger, leave in the name of Jesus.
Depression, leave in the name of Jesus.
Victimization, leave in the name of Jesus.
Soul ties, leave in the name of Jesus.
Powerlessness, leave in the name of Jesus.
Repetition of making the same bad decisions, leave in the name of Jesus.
Addiction to abuse (taking it or giving it), leave in the name of Jesus.
Spousal abuse, leave in the name of Jesus.
Sexual abuse, leave in the name of Jesus.
Child abuse, leave in the name of Jesus.
Mental abuse, leave in the name of Jesus.
Bullying, leave in the name of Jesus.
Physical abuse, leave in the name of Jesus.
Employer abuse and exploitation, leave in the name of Jesus.
Segregation, leave in the name of Jesus.
Discrimination, leave in the name of Jesus.
Abusive banking systems and lending institutions, leave in the name of Jesus.
Abusive penal systems, leave in the name of Jesus.

Blessings, return.
Vindication, return.
Ability to put the bad people out of our lives, return.
Discernment, return.

Father, I ask in the name of Jesus, to please free our family line from abuse. Please free us from being victims of abuse. Please free us from being abusers.

Lord Jesus, many African-Americans have endured an abusive history in this country. Lord, please remove the historical cloak of abuse off the backs of every African-American family in this nation.

I take the cloak of abuse off me, and my family line, in the name of the Father, and the Son, and the Holy Ghost (physically motion to take off a cloak), in Jesus' name.

Please keep this curse of abuse Lord, off me, off my children, and off my children's children, for a thousand generations. Please grant my family line the power to confront abuse when we encounter it, and to walk away when we cannot defeat it. Please give us the courage, Lord, to say "NO MORE!". In Jesus' name. Amen.

www.historyonthenet.com/Slave_Trade/slave_auction.htm

14. ADULTERY

Father, in the name of Jesus, I ask that You would please remove the curse of adultery off my family line.

I cut, break, and sever, all ties to the curse of adultery off my family line, in the name of Jesus of Nazareth.

Lord, I choose to forgive myself (if applies) for committing the sin of adultery.
Please forgive me Lord for participating in this sin.
I choose to forgive my spouse (if applies) for cheating.
Please forgive him Lord for participating in this sin.
I choose to forgive my children (if applies) or my grandchildren (if applies) for committing adultery.
I choose to forgive my mother (if applies) or my father (if applies) for committing adultery, my uncles, my aunts, or my cousins for committing adultery.
I choose to forgive my grandparents on my mother's side and my father's side (if applies) for engaging in the sin of adultery.
I forgive my maternal great-grand parents, and my paternal great-grand parents if they committed adultery.
I choose to forgive my great-great-grandparents on both sides of my family tree, if they committed adultery, and my great-great-great-grandparents on both sides if they committed adultery.

I forgive the slave masters that committed adultery with my slave family members, and I forgive the family members that were forced to participate in adulterous acts, for survival. Whether consensual or non-consensual, the acts of adultery that were put upon my family line (black or white), formed this curse, and I apologize for any family member who introduced this curse, and all those that participated in the sin of adultery, willingly or unwillingly. I repent and ask that You Lord would forgive us all for our participation in this sin.

Please cleanse us Lord from the curse of adultery, as well as the proclivity to be drawn to adulterous actions.
Please nip in the bud, the little actions that start the ball rolling toward adultery,
the looks,
the smiles,
the intimate touching,
the inside jokes,
the sexual innuendos,
the sexy clothes,
the texting,
the emails,
the private meetings,
the lust,
the desire,

the vulnerability,
the power,
the wanting of what's not ours,
the excuses,
the attraction to cheating,
the cheating,
the false justification,
the explanation,
the guilt,
the no guilt,
the inability to stop….and so forth Lord.
Please Jesus, stop all that madness!

I don't know where the curse of adultery started in our family, Lord, but I ask that You would cancel all adulterous acts my family members committed. From me, to my children, and to my children's children, to a thousand generations, I ask that You would please sanctify our relationships and remove our desire for sexual encounters with others.

Adultery, leave.
Betrayal, leave.
Anger, leave.
Insecurity, leave.
Sadness, leave.
Generational family involvement in adultery, leave.
Soul ties, leave.
Generational sexual sin patterns, leave.
Abandonment, leave.
Emotional isolation, leave.
Inability to connect, leave.
 Loneliness, leave.
Joylessness, leave.
Controlling, leave.
Selfishness, leave.
Needing attention, leave.
Desperation, leave in the name of Jesus.

Fidelity, return.
Love, return.
Respect, return.
Healthy relationships, return.
Trust, return.
Intimacy, return.

All in the name of the One, Who can make all things possible, Jesus Christ of Nazareth. Amen.

15. AGAINST US PROFITING FROM OUR AGRICULTURE

Father, in the name of Jesus, I ask that You would please remove the curse against us profiting from our agriculture, off my family's farm.

I cut, break, and cancel all ties to the curse against us profiting from our agriculture, off my family line and my family's farm, in the name of Jesus of Nazareth.

I stand in the gap for anyone in my family line, whether in America, Africa, Europe, or any other continent, that insulted You, bringing a curse on our land for things not to grow. I humbly apologize for their actions, and I repent for what they did. I'm sorry for any sinful deeds against You, including any idol worshipping, bloodletting or blood sacrifices, putting curses on other people's land or properties, or practicing witchcraft.

In the name of Jesus, I choose to forgive my family members for bringing this curse on our family line. I also choose to forgive all those outside my family line, who prevented my family members from profiting from our agriculture.

Idol worshipping, leave in the name of Jesus.
Bloodletting and blood sacrifices, leave in the name of Jesus.
Curses on other people's land, cattle or properties, leave in the name of Jesus.
Witchcraft, leave in the name of Jesus.
Stubborn pride, leave.
Blaming others, leave.
Trumped up charges, leans and taxes, leave in the name of Jesus.
All backroom deals against our land and businesses, leave in the name of Jesus.
All unfair levies and unfair business deals between our family farms and the town, city, county, state or federal government, that white farmers don't have to deal with, leave in the name of Jesus.
Bias business deals, plots to ruin our agriculture and confiscate our land, leave in the name of Jesus.
All attempts to steal our land, please fail in the name of Jesus.
Hidden partnerships against our farms, especially among our own family members, cease in the name of Jesus.

Lord, please let things grow on our farms, homes, neighborhoods, and fields.
Lord, please bless our land to bring prosperity to everyone in our family and to others.
Lord, unless it's Your will, please don't allow us to lose our land or productivity. In fact, we pray You would return, what the locusts have eaten.
Please Lord Jesus, return good produce. Return good harvests. Please restore a great reward for our labor, a thousand fold. In Jesus Christ's name. Amen.

http://www.rolandsmartin.com/blog/index.php/2010/02/19/roland-tjms-02-19-10-roland-s-martintom-joyner-morning-show-roland-talks-with-john-boyd-founder-of-the-national-black-farmers-association/

16. ALCOHOLISM

Father, in the name of Jesus, please remove the curse of alcoholism off my family line.

I cut, break, and sever all ties to the curse of alcoholism, off my family line.

Lord, I choose to forgive the family member that brought this curse onto our family line. And I choose to forgive the circumstances in which the family member began drinking, even if it was to cope with the horrific life of slavery or abuse through the centuries. In the name of Jesus, I sever and burn all roots to what drove my family to drink.

I humbly come before Your throne, repenting for the deeds of the family member that initiated this curse, and I apologize Lord for what they did. Please forgive them, and all members of our family that were addicted to alcohol. Please remove, not only the curse, but all that the curse inflicted on our family line.

I choose to forgive all family members that were alcoholics (list each one and forgive them).

Generational roots to excessive drinking, leave in the name of Jesus.
Generational drinking patterns, leave in the name of Jesus.
Alcohol as a coping tool, leave in the name of Jesus.
Unloved feelings, leave.
Hatred, leave.
Self-hatred, leave.
Abuse, leave.
Denial, leave.
Co-dependency, leave.
Need for numbing, leave.
Selfishness, leave. Pent up anger, leave. Powerlessness leave. Secrets, leave. Jealousy, leave. Comparing, leave. Competition, leave. Being the only caregiver, leave. Being the only bread winner, leave. Being the only sane person in the family, leave. Not having others to help share responsibility, leave. Being controlled, leave. Being controlling, leave. Bad environments, leave. Bad friends, leave. Loneliness, leave. ALL LIES WE'VE GENERATIONALLY BELIEVED, LEAVE IN JESUS' NAME.

Contentment return. Joy return. Hope return. Compassion return. Love return. Self-love return. Self-control return. Discipline return. Dependence on the Holy Spirit return.

Lord I ask that You would please close the door on my family's addiction to alcohol from the time it was introduced to our family line, to me, to my children, and to my children's children for a thousand generations. In Jesus' name. Amen.

17. ALWAYS NEEDING A VILLIAN IN MY LIFE

Father, in the name of Jesus I come before Your throne, asking that You would please remove the curse of me always needing a villain in my life.

I pray to Thee, please forgive me for always casting people into roles in my life, where they serve as the enemy of my soul.

Please forgive me for villianizing things people say or do, to make myself look like the victim.

Please let me see these incidences as simple roadblocks in my life, and not major drama. My life is not a TV show.

I now cut, break, and sever all ties to the curse of always needing a villain in my life, in the name of Jesus. I cancel Lord, the power I've been giving these villains in my life.

While it is true, everyone in my life is not my friend, and everyone in my life is not looking out for my best interest, may the removal of this curse, make me see people as You see them.

Show me how to deal with true enemies in my life. And please show me how to let them go, emotionally, as well as physically.

Please forgive me Lord, for giving too much power to (list all people and organizations in your life you've labeled as your villains).

Please forgive me for empowering them.

Teach me how to call out people who are against me. Help me to be confrontational, when I need to be. And silent when You want me to be.

Help me to pray for those who wish me harm, sending blessings their way.

Teach me Lord, not to weigh myself down, with the burden of being a victim.

Teach me Lord, how to resolve my issues, and keep on stepping.

Teach me Lord, not to make an excuse for people's rude behavior, but recognize it, forgive it, call it out, and if reconciliation is possible, make it happen.

Teach me Lord, to write down the "drama" in my life on paper, and write a book, instead of perpetuating my stories verbally, where the endings always result in me being a victim.

Grant me the ability to problem solve, so my stories are not about me being a victim, but a victor, in Christ. May my stories help others learn how to be survivors too and bless them when they come across their own stories of difficulty.

Please forgive the family member that introduced this curse to our family line. Please forgive the perpetrators outside our family, who victimize us. I choose to forgive both.

Though our stories of victimization are true Lord, we no longer want to live the lives You've given us, as victims.

Victimization, leave in the name of Jesus.
Casting people as villains in my life, leave in the name of Jesus.
Addiction to drama in my life, leave in the name of Jesus.
Helplessness, leave.
Hopelessness, leave.
Anger, leave.
Jealousy, leave.
Arrogance, leave.
Insecurity, leave.
The need to always be right, leave.
Being overly sensitive, leave.
Holding grudges, leave in the name of Jesus.
Not letting go of the past, leave in the name of Jesus.
Not moving on, leave in the name of Jesus.

Discernment, return.
Forgiveness, return.
Problem solving, return.
Courage, return.
Self-confidence, return.
Fairness, return.
Happy endings, return.
Joy, return.
Love, return.

No more villains, Lord.
Heroes!
No more victims, Lord.
Conquerors.!

May we live.
May we survive.
May we thrive!

In Jesus' holy name. Amen!

18. AM I BLACK ENOUGH?

Father, in the name of Jesus, I ask that You would please remove the curse off my family line, of feeling we're not "black enough" for other people.

I cut, break and sever all ties to the curse of feeling I'm not black enough for others, in the name of Jesus.

I don't know when this curse was first introduced to my family line. I don't know if a family member taunted or ridiculed others for not being black enough. I don't know if someone in my family line, through their own pain and jealousy called other slaves, "uncle toms" for catering to their masters. I don't know if my family members were so bitter, that they put other blacks down for not upholding the cause of freedom.

Whatever the case, please forgive my family's judgments, Lord, in Jesus' name. I repent and I apologize to You Lord, on their behalf. I'm sorry for every time they ridiculed other blacks for not being black enough. I also choose to forgive anyone in my family line, including myself (if applies) for judging other blacks.

I pray our family would not fall back into ridiculing others on how they live. I pray that the words that come out of my mouth, and my children's mouths, would be those of encouragement, and not judgment. I pray that my family line would be less critical of how others live, and would be more concerned about how we're living for You.

That said Lord, I choose to forgive others for questioning the blackness of me or my family. Please remove my pre-occupation with the judgments, comments, and criticisms of others about me or my family. I pray the burden of being accepted by others, be removed from me and my family line. I pray we'd only be worried about pleasing You.

I pray You would remove the constant hurt of other people's judgments. I pray You Lord would install in our generation line, a confidence that cannot be shaken. May others' opinions not crush our souls.

Insecurity leave. Pain leave. Burden of being accepted, leave. Self-loathing leave. Jealousy leave. Sadness leave. Loneliness leave. Desperation to be loved, leave.

Ridiculing stop, in the name of Jesus. Thick skin, develop. Laughter, replace sorrow. Joy, replace pain. Identity through my culture, be redefined by my identity in Christ.
Am I black enough?
Wrong question.
Am I God's enough?
Help me to be so, Lord. In Jesus' name. Amen.

19. ANIMOSITY BETWEEN FATHERS and THEIR CHILDREN

Father God, I come before Your throne to share the complexity of the relationship I have with my father. One in which my father loves me, and yet at the same time, it feels like he hates me.

In the name of Jesus, I cut, sever, and break all ties to the curse of animosity that my father has toward me. I sever all his connectors to me that push my buttons, and drive me to do self-destructive things.

I choose, in the name of Jesus, to forgive all his ridiculing comments, criticisms, accusations, disappointments, or comparisons. I choose to forgive his inability to be proud of me, to be happy for me, or his inability to comfort me when I need to be comforted or encouraged.

I forgive all his negative comments, especially when I'm looking for his compliments, support, kindness, encouragement, congratulations, or just plain love.

I choose to forgive his competition with me, his jealousy of me, his anger and frustration with me, his inability to see me as his own child, and not just as my mother's child (who may have hurt him), or, only seeing me as the image of himself (where he's constantly reminded of his own failures).

I choose to forgive him for not being around when I needed him (even if he was working for the good of the family).

I choose to forgive him for abandoning me, or being hostile toward me, especially when he was tired or frustrated with his job or his personal life.

I choose to forgive him every time he made me feel unwanted.

I choose to forgive him for leaving me with people who hurt me, or I forgive him for putting me in harmful situations where I was hurt (alone at home or with a predator).

I choose to forgive him for keeping my mother out of my life (due to their awkward relationship), or refusing to have a peaceful relationship with my mother.

I forgive him for giving me the responsibility of raising myself, alone, or raising my siblings alone, or requiring me to be the caretaker of the family.

I forgive him for requiring me to be his caretaker, where his needs came before my own.

I forgive myself, for loving and hating my father at the same time and I forgive everyone in my family line that perpetuated this curse.
I ask that You would forgive us all Lord, and I give You Lord, every ounce of the complexity of our relationships with our fathers.
I ask Lord that You would heal me of the wounds from this curse.
I ask Lord that You would stop every negative reaction that I commit, out of my woundedness, like over-eating, drinking, or taking drugs to deal with my pain.
I now break those addictions off me, in the name of Jesus.

I ask that You would see to it Lord, that I receive the proper treatment to conquer the negative patterns in my life, as a result of my complex relationship with my father.

Animosity for my father, leave in the name of Jesus.
Pain, leave. Guilt, leave. Anger, leave. Abandonment, leave. Fear, leave. Helplessness, leave. Shame, leave. Bitterness, leave. Self-hatred, leave. Night Terrors, leave. Mistrust, leave.

Healthy father figure, return.
Joy, return.
Trust, return.
Love, return.

I'm not asking Lord, that You remove my father from my life, in order that I may be healed.
I'm asking for a miracle. That You would restore my father's love for me, and my love for him, enabling us to love each other, as You love us. Please disconnect all our past hurts, and fill me with a love that surpasses all understanding when I'm around him.

If, however, it's a case of incest, I am free to give him to You Lord, and free to let my relationship with my father go, in Jesus' name. Also, if being around my father is impossible, or he is deceased, please grant me Lord, an understanding of him and a peace without him, which surpasses all understanding.

It may have started in my family line, with our slave fathers being afraid to love their children, due to the constant threat of their offspring being sold. If this is true, Lord, I break this curse at its root, canceling all father/child animosity off my family line.
I choose to forgive all masters who sold or threatened to sell my ancestors' offspring.
I choose to forgive all fathers in my family line who choose to emotionally distance themselves from their children, rather than to love them unconditionally.

I break this curse off everyone in my family line, from me, to my children, and to my children's children, for a thousand generations. In Jesus Christ's name. Amen!

20. ANIMOSITY BETWEEN MOTHERS and THEIR CHILDREN

Father, in the name of Jesus, I come before Your throne, and I confess the complex relationship I have with my mother. One in which my mother loves me, and yet it feels like she hates me.

In the name of Jesus, I cut, sever, and break all ties to the curse of animosity that my mother has toward me. I sever all her connectors to me that push my buttons, and make me do self-destructive things.

I choose to forgive all her ridiculing comments, criticisms, accusations, disappointments, or comparisons. I choose to forgive her inability to be proud of me, to be happy for me, or her inability to comfort me when I need to be comforted or encouraged.

I forgive all her negative comments, especially when I'm looking for her compliments, support, kindness, encouragement, congratulations, or just plain love.

I choose to forgive her competition with me, her jealousy of me, her anger and frustration with me, her inability to see me as her own child, and not just as my father's child (who may have hurt her), or only seeing me as the image of herself (where she's constantly reminded of her own failures).

I choose to forgive her for not being around when I needed her (even if she was working for the good of the family).

I choose to forgive her for abandoning me, or being hostile toward me, especially when she was tired or frustrated with her job, life, or personal relationships.

I choose to forgive her every time she made me feel unwanted.

I choose to forgive her for leaving me with people who hurt me, or I forgive her for putting me in harmful situations where I was hurt (alone at home or with a predator).

I choose to forgive her for keeping my father out of my life (due to their awkward relationship), or refusing to have a peaceful relationship with my father.

I forgive her for giving me the responsibility of raising myself, alone, or raising my siblings alone, or requiring me to be the caretaker of the family.

I forgive her for requiring me to be her caretaker, where her needs came before my own.

I forgive myself, for loving and hating my mother at the same time and I forgive everyone in my family line that perpetuated this curse. I ask that You would forgive us all Lord, and I give You Lord, every ounce of the complexity of our relationships with our mothers.

I ask Lord that You would heal me of the wounds from this curse. I ask Lord that You would stop every negative reaction that I commit, out of my woundedness, like over eating or drinking, or other self-medicating, to cope with my pain.

I now break those addictions off me, in the name of Jesus. I ask that You would see to it Lord, that I receive the proper treatment to conquer the negative patterns in my life, as a result of my complex relationship with my mother.

Animosity for my mother, leave in the name of Jesus.
Pain, leave. Guilt, leave. Anger, leave. Abandonment, leave. Fear, leave. Helplessness, leave. Bitterness, leave. Self-hatred, leave. Night Terrors, leave. Mistrust, leave.

Healthy mother figure, return.
Joy, return.
Trust, return.
Love, return.

I'm not asking Lord, that You remove my mother from my life, in order that I may be healed. I'm asking for a miracle. That You would restore my mother's love for me, and my love for her. Please give me the love You have Lord, that will enable me to love my mother, without the stings of her comments or actions. Please disconnect all her past judgments of me Lord, and fill me with a love that surpasses all understanding when I'm around her. Please restore our relationship, Lord, with love and patience for one another.

If being around her is impossible, or she is deceased, please grant me Lord, an understanding of her and a peace without her, that surpasses all understanding.

It may have started in my family line, with our slave mothers being afraid to love their children, due to the constant threat of their offspring being sold. If this is true, Lord, I break this curse at its root, canceling all mother/child animosity off my family.
I choose to forgive all masters who sold or threatened to sell my ancestors' offspring.
I choose to forgive all mothers in my family line who choose to emotionally distance themselves from their children, rather than to love them unconditionally.

I break this curse off everyone in my family line, from me, to my children, and to my children's children, for a thousand generations. In Jesus Christ's name. Amen!

David Ritz, "Tributes – Etta James" *Rolling Stones Magazine* 16 February 2012

21. ANXIETY

Father, in the name of Jesus, I ask that You would please remove the curse of anxiety off my family line.

I cut, break, and sever all ties to the curse of anxiety off my family line, that could have started with the horrors of our abduction from our homeland, to our incarceration in holding cells of no return, to our exportation on repugnant slave ships, to the enslavement of my family members.

I stand in the gap of my family line, and I cancel all the anxiety from those events off my family line, in the name of the Son of the living God, Jesus Christ.

Lord I ask that You would forgive all known and unknown parties (people, companies, governments) responsible for initiating this curse on my family line.

I choose to forgive all unknown parties responsible for this family curse. I forgive the abduction of my family from their homeland. I forgive the incarceration of my family members in holding cells of no return. I forgive the exportation of my family members in repugnant slave ships. I forgive the enslavement of my family line for decades. I forgive all anxiety connected to racial inequality that my family line experienced, up to today.

I apologize for those in my family line (white or black) that participated in inflicting anxiety on others, inside or outside my family line. I repent for their behavior, Lord.

I choose to forgive all known parties that are responsible for bringing anxiety on to my family line. (List all persons and events where a tremendous amount of anxiety was brought on your family members. Ask God to forgive them and then you forgive them. Ask God to forgive you, if you've put undue pressure on people, causing them anxiety.)

Lord, I ask You to please free my family from the grips of anxiety. In the name of Jesus, I cancel all anxiety attached to generational memories of horrible events experienced by our family line. By the power of Jesus Christ, I cancel all neuroses, all psychoses, and all phobias tied to the past hurts, that were then passed down our generational line.

Lord Jesus, I choose to trust You. I give You all my mistrust and need to control. Anxiety, leave in the name of Jesus. Fear, leave in the name of Jesus. Depression, leave. Anger, leave. Past failures, leave. Needing to control everything, leave.

Faith in Jesus, return. Forgiveness for all those who let me down, return.
Trust in the Lord, return. Peace, return. Lord, please restore mental health, back to my family line. Lord, please restore peace to me, my children, and my children's children, for a thousand generations, in Jesus' name. AMEN!

22. APATHY

Father, in the name of Jesus, please break the curse of apathy off my family line.

I cut, break, and sever all ties to the curse of apathy off my family line and myself. I cancel all apathy I have towards life. Lord, I know what I need to do, but I constantly feel like <u>not</u> doing it.

I stand in the gap of my family line and I ask that You'd forgive anyone in my family line that brought this curse of apathy on our family.

I ask that You'd forgive all persons involved in cultivating apathy in my family line. Be it from kidnapping my family members from Africa, or from exporting them in slave ships, or from turning my family into chattel, huddling them, selling them, then branding them. I choose to forgive it all. If the apathy came from the generations of barbaric enslavement of my family, or from unjust laws or unequal treatment put upon my family line, I choose to forgive it all.

Lord, I stand in the gap of my family line, and I choose to forgive each and every offender and offense. (Insert any family history you know of, that could have contributed to apathy in your family. Name it, ask God to forgive it, and then you forgive it.)

I forgive the results of apathy, from the time it was first introduced to my family line, to every generation that it hurt, including my grandparents, my parents, me, and my children.

Lord I thank You for removing apathy from our family line, and I ask that You would please restore renewed interest in places where our family has given up.

I give You all fear, all sadness, all depression, all guilt, all slothfulness, all lack of energy, all lack of motivation, and all haranguing of others.

Apathy, leave.
Distractions, leave.
Excuses, leave.
Worry, leave.
Insults and ridicule from others, leave.
Doubts, LEAVE in the name of Jesus.

Lord, would You please restore my energy and passion for my projects, in the name of Jesus Christ of Nazareth.

And Lord, would You please bring into completion, every accomplishment You've designed for my life, my children's lives, and my children's children's lives, for a thousand generations. In Jesus' holy name. Amen.

23. BAD BANKING and MORTGAGES

Father, in the name of Jesus, I ask that You would please remove the curse of bad banking off our family line.

I cut, break and sever, all ties to the curse of bad banking off me and my family line. Lord, I choose to forgive all those in my family that willingly or unwillingly participated in bad banking.

I choose to forgive the member that initiated this curse on our family line, and I humbly apologize for that ancestor (white or black) that conned people out of their money. I repent for all their wrong doing, and I ask that You would forgive us.

I apologize for the people in my family line, that conducted bad money dealings with others (list those you know, and forgive).

I choose to forgive all banks that stole from our family (list all banks and mortgage companies, list what they did to your family, and forgive them). I forgive all deceptive bankers and lenders. I forgive all rude bankers, lenders, tellers and managers. I forgive all banks and lending institutions that were bias against lending to my family or any other African-American family or business. I choose to forgive all history of foreclosures in our family's history.

I choose to forgive myself and all family members (list them) that have poor banking skills. I choose to forgive myself and any family member that mismanaged money. I forgive myself and any family member who trusted corrupted banks and lending institutions and were ripped off. I forgive myself and any family member who didn't adhere to the banks' or lending institutions' directions, rules or guidelines, which allowed penalties and loss of our family's money. I forgive all banks and lending institutions for granting grace to the rich, but not to the poor. I break all patterns of favorable biasness toward the rich, in the name of the Father, and the Son and the Holy Ghost. Lord we pray that the rules, the less wealthy have to follow, would be the same rules the wealthy have to follow. We pray for fairness in the banking world, and in the lending world, in the name of the Father and the Son and the Holy Spirit.

Bad banking, leave, in the name of Jesus. Bad lending, leave. Outrageous penalties, leave. Backroom deals where decisions to alienate the poor, leave in the name of Jesus! Greed, leave. Confusion, leave. Manipulation, leave. Lying, leave. Desperateness, leave. Bad credit, leave. Foreclosures, leave. Leans, leave.

Fair banking, return. Quality banking, return. Good credit, return. Long and fruitful accounts, return. Lord, I renounce the curse of bad banking and bad mortgages off my family line, in Jesus' name. I ask that this curse be removed from not only our family's generational line, but from me, my children, and my children's children for a thousand generations. In Jesus' holy name. Amen.

24. BAD BUSINESS

Father, in the name of Jesus, I ask that You would please remove the curse of bad business from my family line.

I cut, sever, and break all ties to the curse of bad business. I humbly apologize for any wrong doings my family members committed that incurred this curse on our family line.
I repent before You Lord, and ask that You would please forgive us and pardon us for all wrong doings.

I choose to forgive all members of my family who dealt with people in an unfair manner. I choose to forgive all the bad deals my family members had a hand in, myself included (list each family member and the bad business they did, ask the Lord to forgive them, then you forgive them).

Now, I come before You Lord, and I choose to forgive all those, who ripped off my family members, or caused them to be a part of any bad business deals. (List all the people and all the bad business deals you know about. Be sure to include yourself, and forgive yourself if you were a part of a bad deal. Be sure to forgive everyone involved, whether it was an innocent mistake or a deliberate mishandling.)

Lord I ask that You would take away the generational shame and guilt from my family line, whether my family lost big, or prospered big from bad deals.

In the name of Jesus, bad business deals leave.
Fear, leave.
Anger, leave.
Blame, leave.
Shame, leave.
Guilt, leave.
Inability to say "NO", leave.
Addiction to risk, leave.
Gambling addiction, leave.
Inability to discern a bad business deal, leave.
Regrets leave, in the name of Jesus.
Double mindedness, leave.
Strife, leave.
Guilt from a bad past, leave.
Wounded past, leave.
Bad patterns, leave.
Stubbornness, leave.
Pride, leave.
Jeopardizing the family finances, leave.
Addiction to start-ups, leave .
Fear of asking questions, leave.

Lying, leave.
Bad advice, leave.
Fear of pulling out of a deal before it's too late, leave.
Forced intimidation, leave.
Bull crap, leave.
Division, leave.
Self-doubt, leave.
Naiveté, leave.
Being a target for dishonest people, leave.

Forgiveness of others, return.
Forgiveness of self, return.
Discernment, return.
Wisdom, return.
Timing, return.
Courage, return.
Ability to say "NO", return.
Ability to ask the right questions, return.
Ability to see people's hidden agendas, return.
The truth about what's really going on with the business, return.
Good opportunity, return.
Good risk, return.
God's clues, return (seeing what no one else sees)
Finances, return.
Common sense, return.
Reminder of all our good investments, return.
Good financial security, return.
Good personal growth, return.
Opportunity to make up for any regrets, return.
Gratefulness, return.
Entrepreneurship, return.
Joy, return.
Restitution, return.
Compensation, return.
Justice prevail, in Jesus' name.

Thank You Lord, for the opportunity of coming to You with this problem. I pray in the name of Jesus, that this problem of bad business, will not reoccur in our family line.

I pray Lord that You would please grant us the blessing of good business, not only for me and my entire family line, but for our children, and our children's children, for a thousand generations.

In Jesus' holy name. Amen.

25. BAD EDUCATION

What qualifies as a bad education Lord? Is it bad students? Is it bad teachers? Is it a poor environment? Is it run down schools? Is it poor teaching materials? Is it peer driven? Is it a poor home life? Is it bad neighborhoods? Is it poor intelligence? Nay. It's not one thing. For we know the best and the brightest have come through these trials, and have overcome triumphantly.

If there is a pattern of bad or poor education in my family's history, and it's due to some curse, I ask Lord that You would please remove it from my family line. In the name of Jesus, I cut, break, and sever all ties to any curse of bad education that is attached to my family line.

And if there's a pattern of bad or poor education in my neighborhood, due to some curse, then as a resident of this neighborhood, I cut, break, and sever all ties to any curse of bad education that's attached to my neighborhood.

And if there's a pattern of bad or poor education in my city, due to some curse, then as a resident of this city, I cut, break, and sever all ties to any curse of bad education that's attached to my city.

And if there's a pattern of bad or poor education in my state, due to some curse, then as a resident and taxpayer of this state, I cut, break, and sever all ties to any curse of bad education that's attached to my state.

And if there's a pattern of bad or poor education in my nation, due to some curse with this country's ill equipped history with the disenfranchised, the lower social economic populous, the voiceless, the powerless, the hungry, the homeless, the historic outlawing of slaves being taught to read and write, the immigrant, the illegal alien, the migrant, the poor rural and urban working class, the underprivileged, the exploited youth, the child laborer, the truant, the special needs student, the misdiagnosed student, the underutilized, the lack of services, the lack of proper resources, the lack of money, under qualified teachers, apathetic teachers, burned-out teachers, underpaid teachers, over-worked teachers, no in-class support, overpaid administrators, over-crowded classrooms, cut-backs in social services, the worse plans with the best intentions, over-spending, waste, school politics, district politics, union politics, city politics, state politics, national politics, gangs, unreasonable parents, drop outs, harassed or bullied students, not enough resources for children with learning disabilities, corrupt school boards, tenured teachers that should quit, racist, classist and apathetic school districts, the lack of public funding, poor pensions plans for teachers, poor health plans for teachers, poor union and administrative support for teachers, the lack of current technical support, stealing, vandalism, the cutting of sports, music, and art, mean teachers, mean students, mean parents, mean administrations, the breakdown of the family, the breakdown of communities, the unprotected, the disengaged, the unmotivated politicians, not enough tax dollars to support our schools, the fear of law suits, the fear of bullies, child molesters in both public and private schools, not enough protection for our students, not enough public safety, and the rise of school shootings, then, as a citizen of the United States of America, I cut, break, and sever all ties to any current or historical curses of bad education that's attached to my nation, in the name of Jesus Christ of Nazareth.

PLEASE BREAK THIS CURSE OFF OUR NATION LORD, IN THE NAME OF THE FATHER, AND THE SON, AND THE HOLY GHOST!

I ask You Lord to please forgive anyone in my family line that brought this curse on, and I choose to forgive them, as well.

Where anyone in my family line (especially white slave masters who fathered slaves, then kept them from reading) who obstructed anyone from receiving a fair and proper education, I repent and ask for forgiveness for their actions, Lord. I choose to forgive them, as well.

Where anyone in my neighborhood obstructed the opportunity for anyone to receive a fair and proper education, I repent and ask for forgiveness for their actions, Lord. I choose to forgive them, as well.

Where anyone in my school district obstructed the opportunity for anyone to receive a fair and proper education, I repent and ask for forgiveness for their actions, Lord. I choose to forgive them, as well.

Where anyone in my city, obstructed the opportunity for anyone to receive a fair and proper education, I repent and ask for forgiveness for their actions, Lord. I choose to forgive them, as well.

Where anyone in my state, obstructed the opportunity for anyone to receive a fair and proper education, I repent and ask for forgiveness for their actions, Lord. I choose to forgive them, as well.

Where anyone in my nation, obstructed the opportunity for anyone to receive a fair and proper education, I repent and ask for forgiveness for their actions, Lord God Almighty.
I choose to forgive them, as well.

To rectify our nation's educational system, seems impossible. But nothing is impossible with You, Lord. So we ask for a miracle, Lord.

Please cancel the curse of bad education off this nation Lord. We humbly ask that You would please grant every (free or private) primary, secondary, graduate and post grad educational system, Your blessing, by restoring what history has taken away, with excellent education in this nation, for all.
In Jesus' name. Amen.

26. BAD HOUSING

Dear Lord, in the name of Jesus, I ask that You would please remove the curse of bad housing, off my family line.

I cut, break, and cancel all ties to the curse of bad housing off our family line. I ask Lord that You would forgive all those who played a part in the history of forcing my ancestors to live in conditions, not of their choosing.

Lord I choose to forgive all those who played a part in the history of forcing my ancestors into bad housing, starting with the kidnapping of my family members in Africa and their initial bad housing being slave camps, slave jails, and detaining fortresses on the African coasts, before they even set foot on a slave ship to America.

Lord, in the name of Jesus, I break the spiritual chains off my ancestors being imprisoned and being held against their wills, as their first known experience of "bad housing".

Next, I break the bad housing curse off my ancestors being imprisoned in chains on the slave ships coming over to America, in the name of Jesus.

I break the curse of bad housing off my ancestors being held in holding containers off the coasts and on the coasts of America before inspection for slave auctions.

I break off the curse of bad housing off my ancestors, once they were sold and housed in various venues throughout the country, as someone's property.

For those members that were resold during slavery, if it applies to my ancestors, I break off all housing in the "nigger jails" that they had to live in, until they were sold again.

I break off the curse of bad slave masters that cursed slaves with poor housing.

Wow Lord, that's a lot of bad housing!

Lord, please break off all bad and poor housing that occurred, during and after the civil war. I break off all bad housing that resulted after my ancestors were freed from slavery, including share cropping shacks and tenement slums.

Lord, I break off the curse of segregated housing, from the birth of this nation, to what still plagues us today.

I break the curse of bad landlords, bad slumlords, and bad farmers who created tenement housing for the poor, be they black, white, or other races.

I break the curse of bad bankers who wouldn't lend money for home improvements for African-Americans.

I break off the curse of "red lining" black neighborhoods, where banks wouldn't lend money or extend credit for homes to owners who live within the "red line" borders.

I break off the historical curse of backroom deals where the fate of minority housing was "pre-determined" by the rich and powerful.

I cancel the curse of being swindled out of any of our land or inherited property.

I cancel the curse of sloppy records, and white counties making clerical mistakes.

I cancel the curse of "in-house" fighting over property and land amongst my own family members.

I cancel, Lord Jesus, family members who refuse to share what's fair (hey Lord, that goes back to even Your time Luke 12:13).

I cancel any and all demonic activity that played into our receiving bad housing, in Jesus' name.

Lord, if anyone in my family or family line, played a part of inviting in evil, in order to receive better housing, Lord, please forgive us. I'm sorry Lord, and I humbly repent for any action my family did in bringing on the curse of bad housing. I apologize Lord for their actions and behavior, and I ask that You would please lift this curse off us, Lord Jesus. I choose to forgive those family members, as well.

May we please now receive good housing, Lord. Good plumbing. Good utilities. Good neighbors. Good locations.

No more drugs in our neighborhood, Lord. Please.
No more gang banging in our neighborhood, Lord. Please.

Lord, please remove all the bad influences from our neighborhoods, so we can live in peace and tranquility.

Please transform our neighborhoods and our streets into great communities.

In the meantime, Lord, if there's something I can do, to make my place a better place, street, and neighborhood, show me the way Lord. Show me, the way.

In the name of the Father, and His Son, Jesus Christ, and the Holy Ghost. Amen.

Charleston's Walking Slave Tour – Fall 2012

27. BAD INVESTMENTS

Lord God, thank You for waking me up this morning, in my right mind. And thank You that You are the Author and Finisher of all life.

Lord, I'm not sure about all the circumstances involving any member of my family that chose to make bad investments with family money, but I humbly come before Your Throne with these family members in mind.

First I must give You all my anger surrounding them and all the loss they caused our family. I also give You my confusion regarding why they chose these bad investments, and I give You any cloaking of family assets…in other words I forgive them for hiding these bad investments, until it was too late.

I break, cancel and burn all curses off my family line related to bad investments. Lord I ask that You would please forgive everyone in my family line that victimized our family, or were victims of bad family investments.

I break, cancel and burn all the carnage that came out of our families' bad investments, all the inheritance that was lost, and the heavy toll it took on family members.

I choose to forgive the bad investors in our family. I choose to forgive all those who gave bad advice on the investments. I choose to forgive all those who stole our family's assets, all those who mismanaged the investments, and all of those that profited from our families' loss.

I choose to give You my anger Lord, against all those that I've just forgiven, and I ask that You Lord would forgive them. I give You any hatred I feel toward them, and I give You Lord my sadness for what could have been, had the investment gone well, or had the investment not been made at all.

I ask You Lord, Giver of life, to take off of our family line any and all resentment and regrets, and I ask Lord that You would show us a new way to invest. A new way to make money and bring prosperity and wealth to our family.

Please break off our family line, any proclivity to listen to hustlers. Please break off our family line, all gullibility. Make us as wise as serpents and peaceful as doves. Show us Lord whom to trust with our money, and family assets. Give us discernment when we're being ripped off, and how to steer clear of ALL con-artists.

Allow us Precious Jesus to be lenders, and not borrowers.
May poverty never be at our doorstep. May we always tithe to You, and help the needy. May we make You proud of us when we see You in glory, as ones that invested in what pleases You most. In Jesus' name. Amen.

28. BAD MARRIAGES

Before the founding of this nation, at the beginning of its roots, those in charge brought wives over for the first six slaves that were here. Subsequently, during the next 300 years Lord, this country has had very little regard for the sanctity of black marriages.

So Lord, in the name of Your Son, Jesus Christ of Nazareth, I ask that You would please break the curse of bad marriages off our family lines.

I cut, break, and sever all ties to the curse of bad marriages off my family line, from Adam and Eve, to the first time my ancestor introduced this curse to our family line, to everyone in my family line that participated in and reactivated this curse, to me, to my children, and to my children's children for a thousand generations.

I ask forgiveness Lord God, for the person(s) responsible for initiating this curse,
be they my African ancestors, my European ancestors, or any other nationality,
be they slave owners that sold off my married family to different plantations
be they slave owners who forced married family members to mate with other slaves,
be they married slave owners who had sex with family members, causing division
be it due to the physical, emotional, and psychological damages of slavery
be it due to the humiliation of the past, or inferiority complexes, or superiority complexes, or imprisonment, hopelessness, powerlessness, or even witchcraft....
     Who knows?
Lord God, whatever caused and continues to cause bad marriages in my family line, I humbly apologize to You for this sin, and ask that You would please forgive all those in my family line that contributed to bad marriages, either willingly or unwillingly.

I also choose to forgive all those that participated in this curse (list each one and forgive them now).

Please forgive me (if applies) for participating in this curse, and I apologize for my part in a bad marriage.

Lord, I ask that You would please restore my marriage, current or future. I ask that the invisible (historic) issues that we've brought to the marriage, that have been fighting against us, be removed in Your Son's name, Jesus. I ask that those historic issues, of us being sold and used as a commodity, be erased by Your hand Lord God. Please allow my family to start anew, with all the Force of the Living God behind us.

So, in the name of Jesus, by the authority invested in me, as a member of this family line, bad marriage, leave my family blood line.
Sadness, leave.
Soul ties, leave.

Powerlessness, leave.
Abuse, leave.
Witchcraft, leave.
Loneliness, leave.
Envy, leave.
Pity, leave.
Jealousy, leave.
Disconnectedness, leave.
Separation, leave.
Insanity, leave.
Inability to connect, leave.
Boredom, leave.
Runaway spirit, leave.
Selfishness, leave.
Hopelessness, leave.
Chronic complaining, leave.
Comparing, leave.
Depression, leave.
Impotence, leave.
Temptation, leave.
Women hoes and men hoes, leave.
Infidelity (unfaithfulness), leave.
Incest, leave.
Poverty, leave.
Unemployment, leave.
Homelessness, leave.
Lack of opportunity, leave.
Lack of good men and women, leave.
Lack of self-confidence, leave.
Lack of means, leave.
Lack of appeal, leave in Jesus' name.

Time for new beginnings, Lord.
Please bring back to my family line, <u>Your</u> original plan of good marriage.
Joy, come.
Love, come.
Hope, come.
Faith, come.
Peace, come.
Patience, come.
Kindness, come.
Goodness, come.
Self-control, come.
Good Companionship, come.
Blessings come, all, in the name of Jesus of Nazareth. Amen and Amen.

DVD: *Slavery and the Making of America,* Director Dante J. James, Director Gail Pellett, Director Chana Gazit, and Director Leslie D. Farrell

29. BAD MEDICINE

Father God, in the name of Your Son, Jesus Christ, I ask that You would please remove the curse of bad medicine off my family line.

I cut, sever, and break all ties to the curse of bad medicine practiced on me and all family members in the history of our lineage.

As a member of this family, I stand in the gap of our family line, and I humbly apologize for the actions of any of my African, European, or Native American ancestors that introduced this curse to our family line. I apologize for any witchcraft that was used to bring healing, or to make someone sick, or to kill them. I repent for any bad testing my family may have performed on people willingly or unwillingly. I repent for any accidental or deliberate medical deaths my family members may have caused. Any kind of medicine that was practiced by my family members, that was not pleasing to You Lord, I apologize for their actions, and I repent for what they did. I know You abhor the practice of evil, and I pray that You would please forgive them of their actions, in the name of Jesus.

I also choose to forgive all members of my family line that practiced bad or evil medicine (list any you know, what they did, and forgive each one).

Lord, I also choose to forgive all doctors, nurses, hospitals, clinics, government agencies, the military, pharmaceutical companies, the academic community, the chemical industry, and any other group of people or companies that used my family as guinea pigs for lab experiments, jeopardizing their health. I choose to forgive all malpractice incidences where my family members were harmed, made sick, or killed, with or without their knowledge, with no power for recourse.

I choose to forgive all doctors, nurses, hospitals, and all people in the medical profession that mishandled any of my family members, including my slave ancestors, my great grandparents, my grandparents, my parents, myself (and siblings), my children, and/or my grandchildren (list any members that were medically mistreated, what happened, and forgive everyone involved).

Fear, leave.
Malpractice, leave.
Anger, leave.
Powerlessness, leave.
Arrogance of doctors, leave.
Bad doctors, leave.
Prejudiced doctors, nurses, and insurances, leave.
Lack of communication, leave.
Mistrust of the medical community, leave.
Fear to ask questions, leave.
Fear to go to the doctor, leave.

I choose to forgive all doctors that misdiagnosed any of my family members, causing any unnecessary harm, mutilations, deficiencies, pain, or death.

Lord, in the name of Jesus, would You please grant our family, good medical care. Please grant us medical discernment. Our Great God, Physician, and Priest, please take away our fear of medicine, and place in our lives good doctors, good hospitals, good nurses, good midwives, good nutritionists, good medicine, good quality of life and excellent health coverage for all Americans.

Please grant us a keen awareness to routinely get checked out, and please put in our path, good people who will look out for our well-being.

If I have family members that won't go to the doctor, please put in their path, good physicians, friends, and social contacts that they trust, to give them good advice on how to live the life You intended them to live.

Lord, please cut out of our lives, any unnecessary suffering!
Please grant us peace of mind, peace of body, and peace of soul, where disease is unable to penetrate us.

Please grant us discernment on where to live, so that pollutants can't harm us. And if we are exposed to any toxicants, ANYWHERE (food, water, air, land), please reveal those toxicants to us, and grant us the POWER, to take care of it, get rid of it, change it, or the ability to move away.

You are all powerful Lord, and it is not Your will that we die before our time. So we place our times in YOUR HANDS. We ask You to please be our guide throughout this life, allowing us to see the invisible and visible pitfalls of unhealthy living, and the strength to avoid them, when possible.

Get us out of unhealthy situations Lord, please remove unhealthy people from our lives. Please put Your loving arms around us, and be our protector Lord Jesus.

Good medicine, return.
Good medical practices, return.
Good medical judgment, return.
Taking care of ourselves, return.
Taking good care of our loved ones, return.
Good doctors, return.
The ability to release things in my life that don't make me healthy, return.
The power to say NO, return.
The power to say YES, return.
The power to change to a healthier environment, return!

Help us Lord. Help us help ourselves, and each other. In Jesus' name. AMEN

30. BEING A BULLY

Lord, I ask that the curse of being a bully be removed from our family line. As a member of this family, I cut, sever, and break all ties to the curse of bullying others, by the blood of Jesus Christ of Nazareth.

I ask You Lord to please forgive the person who initially brought this curse on our family line. Whether it was initiated by the white, black, African, Native American or European side of my family, I choose to forgive that family member and all other persons in my family line that participated in bullying people. I humbly ask You Lord to please forgive all those in my family line that participated in this curse.

Lord, I am sorry that I am a bully (if applies). I repent for my actions. I apologize for making people feel small and threatened, whether they deserved it or not. Please forgive me for teasing people, making them feel small, in order to make myself feel better. Please forgive me for teasing or bullying my family members. Please forgive me for teasing or bullying my neighbors or friends. Even if I was just joking, I was still wrong. (take this time out to think of the people you've bullied and apologize for every person you hurt, before the Lord). I repent for every person I hurt, and I ask for Your forgiveness Lord, God Almighty.

Being a bully, leave.
Teasing, leave.
Jealousy, leave.
Feelings of being insignificant, leave.
Hostility, leave.
False sense of empowerment, leave.
Joy from other's humiliation, leave.
Shame, leave.
Powerlessness, leave.

Forgiveness, return.
My Personal Significance, return.
True joy, return.

I choose to forgive those people in my life that made me feel unworthy, that perpetuated my bullying behavior. I choose to forgive them (mom, dad, siblings, friends, teachers, grandparents) right now (forgive each person and incident where you were bullied).

I thank You Lord, for the healing that You are doing in me, to heal me from this disposition. When confronted with obstacles, or annoying people, I give Your Holy Spirit permission to step in and calm my temper, every time. I may not get my behavior under control every time, but I ask You Lord for the tools to stop this behavior, so that I may not cause any more unnecessary pain. In Jesus' name. Amen.

31. BEING A CRUEL TASK MASTER

Father, in the name of Jesus, please remove the curse of being cruel task masters, off my family line, whether it started here in America, Africa, Asia or Europe.

I cut, sever, and break off all curses off my family line where we were the task masters, being verbally abusive, physically brutal, and tactically inhuman to our fellow man.

This curse may have been introduced to our family line, all the way back to Egypt, or any other African, Asian or European empire, where my ancestors held groups of people in massive slavery. For this Lord, I repent and apologize. This curse may have been introduced to our family by my white side of the family, where my ancestors beat, raped, butchered, or enslaved their fellow man. For this Lord, I repent and apologize.

Please forgive all those in my family line who enslaved, beat, persecuted, oppressed, burned, tortured, maimed or killed people, whether they were ordered to do so, or not. I choose to forgive all my family members who participated in such actions, in the name of Jesus.

Of the family members that I know were cruel, I bring their cruelty before Your throne, and ask for Your forgiveness Lord. (Start listing every family member you know of, that was cruel…like your grandmother, mom or dad for excessively screaming or beating you, or others. Ask God to forgive them. Then you forgive them.)

If I have participated in being a cruel taskmaster, Lord, abusing my authority over others, including my family, I humbly apologize for all my actions, and ask that You would please forgive me (list the times you were cruel, repent and ask God to forgive each time). Help me to be a better boss. Effective, without humiliating others. To be fair and just, without taking my frustration out on my staff, family, or friends. And when something isn't working out, help me to resolve the problem, without cruelty. Help me to sustain compassion and reason, in all circumstances.

Cruelty, leave. Anger, leave. Sadness, leave. Powerlessness, leave. Insecurity, leave. Stress, leave. Unmet expectations, leave.

Peace, return. Joy, return. Smart goals, return. Achievable goals, return. Fairness, return. Encouragement, return. Camaraderie, return.

In the future, Lord Jesus, I pray for myself and for our family, that we will be good people with authority, who will not demonstrate cruelty, but will provide safe, fair, and productive environments for our employees, work force, constituents, patients, students, and/or family members…for a thousand generations.

32. BEING A FATHER WHO ABANDONS

Father, in the name of Jesus, I stand in the gap of my family, asking for forgiveness for all the fathers in my generational line, who abandoned their children, physically, mentally, or emotionally.

Please Lord, remove the curse of father abandonment off our family line.

Lord I break, sever, and cut all ties to the curse of father abandonment in my family line, and I forgive all those that participated in leaving their children willingly or unwillingly.

I ask Lord that You would please forgive the family member that introduced this curse to our family. I repent and apologize to You Lord, for his actions and for every other father's actions who abandoned our family line.

I choose to forgive all the damage they caused our family line. I choose to forgive (name each abandoning father), and I choose to forgive the circumstances which caused them to leave (name each event and forgive).

Please forgive me (if applies) Lord for abandoning my own children (List each time you abandoned your children. Even if it was for a good reason). I repent and apologize to You for my actions in abandoning my family.

I choose to forgive all fathers and father figures that abandoned me (if applies). I choose to forgive myself (if applies) for abandoning others.

I choose to forgive You Lord (if applies), because I believed You abandoned me when others abandoned me, too.

Of course this is impossible. So I choose to see that in my life You never left me. Please forgive my doubt, and please bring healing to the father relationships in my family line.

I choose to forgive all abandoning fathers, from the beginning of my family line, all the way to the time fathers in my ancestry were abducted from Africa to be slaves in America.

I choose to forgive our kidnappers and slave traders that disenfranchised our homes in Africa.

I choose to forgive the slave sellers and the masters that bought our fathers,
then insisted that our fathers breed,
then sold off our fathers,
or sold off their wives
or sold off their children.

Lord I cancel all the damage that was done by slave trading and breeding, to create an institution of abandonment by black fathers.

I cancel all curses on my family line, where fathers chose not to care about their offspring, as a means of coping with the loss of their children.

Abandonment (physical, mental or emotional), leave.
Hopelessness, leave.
Powerlessness, leave in the name of Jesus.
Despair, leave.
Depression, leave.
All avoidance of feelings as a means of coping, leave.
The generational curse of being a stud, leave in the name of Jesus.
All hate and self-hate, leave in the name of Jesus.
All guilt and shame be recognized, forgiven, and leave in the name of Jesus.
All excuses to stay away from the family, leave in the name of Jesus.
All inability to manage our lives, leave.
All inability to manage our money, leave.
All inability to maintain jobs, leave.
All inability to control our appetites, leave.
All inability to love our children, leave.
All inability to keep our relationships, leave.
All inability to keep our homes, leave.
All inability to stay healthy, leave.
All inability to worship You, Lord, leave in the name of Jesus and may we be restored by the power of Your cross.

Good parenting, return.
Time with the family, return.
Stability, return.
Management of time, return.
Joy, return.
Concentrating on what matters, return.
Good employment, return.
Money, return.
Prosperity, return.
Encouragement, return.
Good fathering, return.
Faithfulness to a committed relationship, return.

Please restore Lord, healthy father relationships in my family line.
Show me how to be a good father, even when I forget to be or don't want to be.

Please restore the father relationship, starting with me, my children, and my children's children for a thousand generations. In Jesus' name. AMEN

33. BEING A MOTHER WHO ABANDONS

Father, in the name of Jesus, I stand in the gap of my family line, asking forgiveness for all mothers in my generational line, who abandoned their children, physically, mentally, or emotionally.

Please Lord, remove the curse of mother abandonment off our family line.

Lord I break, sever, and cut all ties to the curse of mother abandonment in my family line, and I forgive all those that participated in leaving their children willingly or unwillingly.

I ask Lord that You would please forgive the family member that introduced this curse to our family.

I repent and apologize to You Lord, for her actions and for the actions of every other abandoning mother in our family line.

I choose to forgive all the damage they caused.

I choose to forgive them (list each abandoning mother, what they did, and forgive) and the circumstances for which they left (list circumstances and forgive).

Please forgive me Lord, for abandoning my children (if applies). I repent for my actions (list each time you abandoned your children, apologize to God, and forgive yourself).

I choose to forgive You Lord, for allowing this to happen to our family line. I may have thought it meant You didn't love us, which is impossible.

I choose to see You never stop loving us, and I choose to forgive all mothers in the family, that seem to not love us.

I choose to forgive any abandoning mother, from the beginning of my family line, to the mothers that were abducted from Africa to be slaves in America.

I choose to forgive the kidnappers and slave traders that disenfranchised our homes in Africa.

I choose to forgive the slave sellers and the masters that bought our mothers, then insisted they breed with men, including the slave masters, then hurt our slave mothers more, by selling them off, or selling their spouses off, or selling their children off.

Lord I cancel all the damage that was done by slavery, institutionalizing the abandonment by mothers.

I cancel all curses on my family line, where mothers chose not to care about their children, as a coping mechanism for their loss.

In the name of Jesus, mother abandonment leave!
Physical and mental abandonment, leave!
Disengaged emotions, leave.
Apathy, leave.
Hopelessness, leave.
Powerlessness, leave.
Despair, leave.
Depression, leave.
All suppressed feelings, as a means of coping, leave.
All exaggeration of feelings as a means of coping, leave.
All hatred of others, leave.
All self-hatred, leave.
All guilt be recognized, forgiven and leave in the name of Jesus.
All shame be recognized, forgiven, and leave, in the name of Jesus.
All excuses to abandon our children, leave in the name of Jesus.
All excuses to stay away from our children, leave in the name of Jesus.
All inability to control:
My money,
My health,
My career,
My appetite,
My children,
My relationships,
My home life,
and whatever else is out of control in my life, all leave, in the name of Jesus.

Please restored my life, by the power of His cross.

Please restore the mother relationships in our family line.

Help me to be a good mother, even when I don't want to be.

Please bring restoration, for my children, and my children's children for a thousand generations.

In Jesus' name. AMEN

34. BEING ABANDONED BY YOUR FATHER

Father God, it seems like the fathers in our family line left us too soon, because of death, divorce, imprisonment, sin, selfishness, the inability of our parents to get along, or painfully, they just didn't want to be with us.

Lord I come to You and ask that You would please remove the curse of being abandoned by fathers, off our family line. I break, cut, and sever all ties to this curse, off my family line, in Jesus' name. Lord, I ask that You would please forgive all the fathers in my family line that abandoned their children, including my father (if applies), physically, mentally, or emotionally.

I choose to forgive all those that contributed to this curse, starting with Adam in the garden of Eden. I break off the curse of the original disconnect between Father and son, when Adam's sin caused You to put him out (Genesis 3:23). I cancel the perpetuation of Adam's broken relationship with his son, Cain (Genesis 4: 6-16). By the blood, shed by Jesus on the cross, the removal of this curse was accomplished on Calvary, and I now lay claim to this victory for my own family line.

I choose to forgive all fathers who abandoned their children, starting from the beginning of my family line, to the time my ancestors were abducted from Africa to be slaves in America. I cancel the abandonment that our African mothers and children felt, when their fathers were stolen. I cancel all the emotional, physical and mental abandonment my kidnapped African family felt, when forced to leave their families behind. I choose to forgive the kidnappers and slave traders that disenfranchised our homes in Africa.

I choose to forgive the slave sellers and the masters that bought our fathers, then insisted our fathers breed with many women, and then sold off our fathers, or our mothers, or their children. Lord I cancel all the damage that was done by slave trading and breeding, creating an institution of children being abandoned by our fathers. I cancel all curses on my family line, where fathers had no choice in leaving their children, and I cancel all generational pain, connected to being abandoned.

I forgive all fathers (list each one) in my family line, who abandoned their children, emotionally, physically, or mentally (list every time they did), including myself (if applies). For every time I was abandoned by my father (list each time), I choose to forgive him (forgive each incident you list).

I cancel all physical, emotional and mental abandonment of fathers. I cancel all ill will, depression, psychosis, anger, self-medicating, hysteria, shame, guilt, self-loathing, jealousy, greed, envy, self-destruction off my family line.

You Lord, are our Father, and You have always loved us. Please re-establish our relationships with our fathers. Please grant us excellent father relationships, even if it's not with our own biological fathers. In Jesus' name. Amen

35. BEING ABANDONED BY YOUR MOTHER

Lord God, I ask that the family curse of mothers in my family, abandoning their children, be removed from my family line. Lord, as a representative of this family, I cut, sever, and break all ties to the curse of being abandoned by mothers, off my family line.

Lord, I humbly apologize for all mothers in my family line that participated in this action, for whatever reason, and ask that You would please forgive all mothers that abandoned their children.

I choose to forgive all the mothers in my family, that were forced emotionally, physically or mentally to abandon their off spring,
from the first mother in my family line who introduced this curse by abandoning her children,
to the abduction of my family members from Africa,
to their lives as slaves in this country,
to the post civil war era,
to the civil rights era,
to today and to myself.

I also forgive all mothers in my family line that choose to abandon their children because of selfishness.

I choose to forgive all those that contributed to this curse, starting with Eve in the garden of Eden, whose sin caused You to put her out (Genesis 3:1-23). I break off this curse of the original disconnect between Parent and daughter. By the blood shed by my Lord Jesus on the cross, the removal of this curse was accomplished on Calvary , and I now lay claim to this victory for my own family line!

Lord, I choose to forgive all mothers who abandoned their children, starting from the beginning of my family line, to the time that our African mothers were abducted from Africa to be slaves in America. I cancel the abandonment that the children from our African families felt, when their mothers were stolen. I cancel all the emotional, physical and mental turmoil our kidnapped African mothers felt, when forced to leave their families behind.

I choose to forgive the kidnappers and slave traders who disenfranchised our family homes in Africa.

I choose to forgive the slave sellers and the slave masters who bought our mothers, pimped our mothers, raped our mothers and dismissed their slave children, not claiming them as their own.

I forgive the slave masters who sold off our mothers and sold off her children, and the enormous psychological damage it placed on our family line.

Lord I cancel all the damage that was done by slave trading and breeding, institutionalizing the culture of abandonment by our mothers, either physically, emotionally or mentally.

I cancel all curses on my family line, where mothers chose not to care about their off-spring in order to cope with their loss.

I cancel mothers minimizing their emotions of having to put their children as secondary, in order to make a living for the family, making their jobs (as slaves or free), primary.

I forgive all mothers (list every relative) in my family line, who left their children emotionally, physically, and mentally lacking (list everything they did and forgive), including myself (if applies).

If I was abandoned by my mom (list each time you were abandoned) I choose to forgive you mom (forgive each incident).

I cancel all physical, emotional and mental abandonment of our mothers.
I cancel all the bad feelings attached to that abandonment.
Abandonment issues, leave.
Sadness, leave.
Depression, leave.
Psychosis, leave.
Anger, leave.
Fear, leave.
Self-medicating, leave.
Outbursts, leave.
Shame, leave.
Guilt, leave.
Self-loathing, leave
Jealousy, leave.
Selfishness, leave.
Self-destruction, leave off my family line, in Jesus' name.

I ask Lord that You would please restore the mother relationships in my family line.
Forgiveness, return.
Joy, return,
Trust, return.
Nurturing, return.
Feeling loved and appreciated, return.

Please grant us Lord, a loving relationship with a mother figure, who can nurture us in a way that's restorative. In Jesus' name. Amen.

36. BEING ATTACKED

Father, in the name of Jesus, I bring before You the curse of being attacked Lord, and I ask that You would please remove this curse from my family line.

As a member of this family, I break, cut and sever all ties of the curse of being attacked off my family line.

Lord, I don't know which family member first introduced this curse to our family line, but I ask for Your forgiveness for whatever they did. I apologize for their actions and repent for their sins. I choose to forgive them, and anyone else in my family (list them and apologize to God) for attacking people.

I now come before You Lord, and ask that You would please protect my family members from being attacked. For all attacks that have come against my family, including the original abduction of my family members from Africa, I choose to forgive and release our captors and perpetrators, in Jesus' name.

Being attacked, leave.
Terror, leave.
Fear, leave.
Being a target, leave.
Depression, leave.
Failure to make sense of things, leave.
Being stuck, leave!
Doubt, leave.
Violent outburst, leave!
Double-mindedness, leave.
Victimization, leave!
Pity, leave!
Broken spirit, leave.

Lord, I ask You to please protect our family members, granting us discernment in our comings and goings. Bless us with the courage to move out of dangerous environments.
I ask You Lord for protection from physical harm, as well as mental harm.

Discernment, return.
Peace, return.
Safety, return.
Joy, return.
Freedom, return.
Renewed spirit, return.

Please keep me safe, as well as my family members safe. I ask this for my children, and my children's children for a thousand generations. In Jesus' name, Amen.

37. BEING BULLIED

Father, in the name of Jesus, I asked that You would please remove the curse of being bullied, off my family line.

I'm not sure being bullied gets more obvious, than being abducted from one's homeland, and being forced to do free labor that benefits another race and society.

I choose to forgive all those that bullied my family into the oppression of slavery. I also ask Lord, that You would forgive our oppressors.

By the power invested in me, as a member of this family, I hereby cancel the curse of bullying off my family line.

I cut, sever and break all ties to the curse of being bullied, off my family, in Jesus' name.

Being bullied, leave.
Fear, leave.
Shame, leave.
Depression, leave.
Anger, leave.
Sadness, leave.
Powerlessness, leave.
Hopelessness, leave.
Suicidal thoughts, leave.
The inability to do anything, leave.
The inability to say anything, leave.
Being a target, leave.
Lack of motivation, leave.
Fault finding, leave.
Overly self-conscious, leave.
Self-blaming, leave.
Feelings of being weak, leave.
Grudges, leave.
A need to pacify others, leave.
Tolerating being bullied, leave.

Courage, return.
Wisdom, return.
Blessings, return.
The ability to speak up, return.
Forgiveness, return.
Confrontation, return.
Truth, return.
Healthy community, return.

Solidarity, return.
Policing, return.
Good policy, return.
Angels protecting us, return and stay!

Father, I choose to forgive all those who bullied me or my family members (list all bullies, what they did to you or your family and forgive each incident.)

I ask that You would empower everyone in our family line, to tell the right people, when we are being threatened. And when we do tell Lord, may action to protect us, happen quickly.

Father, I choose to give You all the lies I believed when I was bullied.
   (Say, I give You Lord, the lie that I'm not strong.
      I give You Lord, the lie that I'm weak.
      I give You Lord, the lie that I'm stupid.
      I give You Lord, the lie that I'm not as popular as most.
      I give You Lord, the lie that I speak poorly.
      I give You Lord, the lie that I'll get hurt if I talk back.
      I give You Lord, the lie that pain follows when I speak up.
      I give You Lord, the lie that the retaliation that I may experience afterwards isn't worth me standing up for my rights.
      I give You Lord, the lie that being bullied isn't that bad. And so on.)

And now Father, I give You all the bad emotions attached to those lies.
I give You my pain, my suffering,
my parents' suffering,
my children's suffering,
my grandparents' suffering,
my great grandparents' suffering,
the suffering and woundedness in my childhood,
my sibling's suffering,
my embarrassment,
and my humiliation.
I give you my loneliness in not being able to tell people I was bullied,
I give You my sorrow when I did tell people I was bullied and people laughed or didn't care, or told me I was a coward and told me to fight.

I give You all my bullies Lord, and I choose to forgive each one (list and forgive). Lord, please release me, and my children, and my children's children from the cycle of bullying, for a thousand generations. In Jesus' name. Amen.

Lord Jesus, I ask that You would help me not to repeat the same offenses that were done to me, on to others. If I have, in turn, become a bully, please forgive me of my offenses and show me where I need to repent and repair relationships. In Jesus' name. Amen.

38. BEING CALLED A NIGGER or OTHER RACIST NAMES

Father, in the name of Jesus, I'm tired of being called a nigger. I can't stop the surprise verbal attacks of being called this name, but I can ask Lord, that You would remove the curse of being called a nigger off my family line, in Jesus' name. I also ask that in the future, Your Spirit would protect me and my family from feeling any pain or hostility when we're called a nigger. I pray that the sting of the word and its perpetrators, would come off as "RIDICULOUS" to us.

I ask Lord that You would forgive this country and its citizens for the history of its use of the word "nigger" and please forgive all the hatred that it has embroiled.

I choose to forgive this country and its citizens for the history of its use of the word "nigger" and other racist names. I choose to forgive all the hatred that the word nigger and other racist names have embroiled (list any historical events you know of like the marches by Dr. Martin Luther King Jr., ask God to forgive those who hatefully used the word, "nigger", then you forgive them).

I cut, break and sever all ties to the curse of being called a nigger and other racist names, off me and my family line. I choose to forgive all those in my family's past, that called me or my family members, niggers (list your family stories, ask God to forgive those who hatefully used the word, "nigger", then you forgive them).

I choose to forgive the person in my family line (white or black), that initiated this curse. I choose to forgive my family and myself (if applies) for using the words nigger or nigga.

Granted, if I use the term nigga (if applies), I don't mean nigger. However Lord, I ask that You would please forgive me for using this term on friends and family, or, using it as a derogatory name for people who upset me.

Lord, I ask that You would remove from me ANY condemnation I have about myself or my fellow blacks. I ask that You would not only remove this condemnation from my mind, but from every area of my soul and spirit.

I ask that You would please help me to fully understand, that You created us all to be beautiful and wonderful in Your sight. For all are Yours, Lord. And it hurts You when we demean anyone in Your creation.

I ask that You would forgive me for labeling anyone a nigger or a nigga. It may be a word I've grown up loving to use it (if applies), although I hate hearing whites use the term to describe blacks (playfully or derogatorily).

The duel complexity of this word, I give to You, Lord. It is not a word You favor. I ask that You would help us all, break the habit of using it.
In Jesus' name. Amen.

39. BEING PLAYED or TRICKED or USED

Father, in the name of Jesus, I ask that You would please remove the curse of being played, tricked, or used off my family line.

I cut, sever, and break all ties to the curse of being played off me and off my family line, in the name of Jesus.

Lord, I ask You to please forgive the family member who initiated this curse on to our family line, by playing, tricking, or using people. Please forgive all those in my family that perpetuated this curse. I apologize and repent for what they did, and I choose to forgive them (black or white) and all their actions (list any events you know about where your family played people, repent on their behalf, then you forgive them).

Lord, forgive me, for every time I played, tricked or used people (list every time you did this, repent, and forgive yourself).

I now choose to forgive the following people and institutions for "playing" our family members, including tribesman from Africa that captured and sold us, the entire American/Europe slave industry; the Founding Fathers that instilled slavery; the Constitution that allowed slavery; the Church for not only tolerating slavery, but using the Bible as an excuse to enslave us; the international merchant community (which slavery helped in developing the middle class) that profited from slavery; the slave masters, owners and the rest, who made promises to my slave ancestors, and never kept them: and all the other psychological warfare this country plagued African-Americans with, throughout the history of this nation.

I choose to forgive, all those in my family's personal history, that played, tricked or used us (list and forgive). I break and cancel all generational agreements and alliances, my family members may have made, while being played and used. I break these agreements, off me and off all those members that came before me, and all those, after me.

I now choose to forgive everyone in my life, who have played, tricked, or used me in the past, either mentally, physically, financially, or romantically (list and forgive).

Lord, I choose to give You my humiliation, sadness and anger in these situations.

Being played, leave in Jesus' name.
Being tricked, leave.
Being used, leave.
Humiliation, leave.
Sadness, leave.
Betrayal, leave.

Rejection, leave.
Feeling of no value, leave in the name of Jesus.
Being a target, leave.
Being a commodity, instead of a human being, leave in Jesus' name.
Being a whipping post, leave.
Being leverage for sordid gain, leave.
Sexually exploited, leave.
Manipulation, leave.
Controlled by others, leave.
Anger, leave.
Fear, leave.
Powerlessness, leave.
Inability to comprehend what's really going on, leave.
Confusion, leave.
Scapegoating, leave.
Blaming, leave.
Not letting go, leave.

Freedom from being played, return.
Wisdom, return.
Discernment, return.
Speaking up, return.
Fighting for our rights, return.
Compensation, return.
Revenge is Yours Lord Jesus, so we stay away from that.
Forgiveness, return.
Justice, return.
Helpfulness, return.
Community, return.
Happiness, return.
Joy, return.
In Jesus' name.

Lord, that's a lot of people and situations to forgive.

But I ask that You would remove the hurt from all those incidences and clear our minds to love and receive love again.

Free me and my family to receive the blessings that have been held back because of the past. Help us to move on from here.

Please keep my family from being played, starting with me, my children, and my children's children, for a thousand generations. In Jesus' name. Amen.

DVD: *Slavery and the Making of America*, Director Dante J. James, Director Gail Pellett, Director Chana Gazit, and Director Leslie D. Farrell
"Slavery in New York" New York Historical Society exhibition, 7 October 2005 - 5 March 2006

40. BETRAYING YOUR OWN PEOPLE

Father, in the name of Jesus, I come before Your throne, asking You to please remove the curse of being a traitor to our own people, off my family line.

Lord, I cut, break, and sever all ties to the curse of being put in the position of betraying other African-Americans, off my family line.

Lord I ask that You would forgive all those in my family line that participated in having to betray other African-Americans, at the threat of whites, blacks or other nationalities.

Lord I choose to forgive those in my family line that sold out other Africans, in the slave trade, or whipped slaves at their masters' command, or fought against the Revolutionists at the British's command, or fought against the Union at the Confederate's command, or restricted blacks during Jim Crow laws, or were non supportive during civil rights, or even something as simple as being pulled into degrading conversations with whites, about blacks, in order to not offend whites.

Lord what does it really mean to be a traitor?
When have we truly offended our race, and sold them out?
When was it all right to do so, in order to protect ourselves and our families?
When was it not all right to do so, and simply selfishness?
When did we betray ourselves, at the expense of our own race and heritage?
When did we help the greater cause by not fighting at all?
When did we fall into the trap of serving the enemy?
And Lord, when was our guilt (or non-guilt) justified?

Lord, there's a Harper's Weekly woodcut caricature of two black men at Yorktown, Virginia in 1862, being pressed by a Confederate soldier to fire on the Union. They would be killed by sharpshooters.

So Lord, in the name of Jesus, I break off my family line, all fear to obey orders (white or black) that betray my race.
I break off all intimidation.
I break off all using me and my family as a buffer or human shield to protect white society from their mistakes OR black society from their mistakes.
I break off all guile and confusion as to whom to protect and whom to serve.
I break off all timidity as to when to speak up or speak out.
I break off all need to be liked, by associates and superiors (of all races), especially when they comment on African-American issues they don't understand.
I break off the need to conform to ideas that are contrary to God's ideas.
I break off all fear to support my own people.
I choose to tear down the emotional wall I've built between myself and other blacks.

I cancel any resistance I have to helping blacks, forgiving those in the past, who were hostile towards me or didn't want my help.
I give You Lord my anger toward any blacks that made me mad, including my own family members.
I break the treacherous social barrier that our society has built, that has pitted blacks against one another, since slavery.
I forgive all attempts by the enemy to pit me against other blacks.
I forgive all attempts by the enemy to sabotage my own freedoms, rights and ability to exert anything in this country that I'm entitled to, especially rights that blacks fought so hard for throughout the history of this nation.

I ask Lord that You would forgive any family member that was not supportive to our own race, but only when it displeased You Lord.
I choose to forgive my family members for any time they became a traitor to other African Americans, but only when it displeased You Lord (list events and forgive).
I choose to forgive myself (if applies), anytime I was not supportive of my own people, but only when it displeased You Lord(list events and forgive).

Being put in the position of betraying my own people, leave in the name of Jesus.
Fear, leave.
Guilt, leave.
Betrayal, leave.
Shame, leave.
Self-doubt, leave.
Anger, leave.
Needing to please whites, leave.
Needing to partner with those who don't have my best interest in mind, leave.
Needing to betray my own, to win favor, leave.

Love, return.
Joy, return.
Discernment, return.
Sharing my opinion, at the right time, return.
Not sharing my opinion, at the right time, return.
Being willing to question people's agendas, when they ask my opinion, return.
God's agenda, return.

Please forgive me when I'm being adversarial to Your cause, Lord.
Please help me to see Your plan in action, then grant me the conviction of my heart to see it through. Show me how I can be supportive of my people and glorify You at the same time.

On the issues where I feel conflicted about helping my people, help me to see my people the way You see my people. Then Lord, please show me what to do, leaning on You at every turn. In Jesus' name. Amen.

41. BEING RIPPED OFF

Father God, in the name of Jesus, I ask that You would please remove the curse of being ripped off, off my family line.

I cut, break, and sever all ties of the curse of being ripped off from my family line.

I apologize and repent for the family member who initiated this curse onto the family and
I ask Lord for their forgiveness. I choose to forgive that family member, as well.

Lord, I repent for every time other family members cheated someone (list, apologize to God on their behalf, then you forgive them), be it money, land, someone's spouse, someone's idea, or someone's honor. I choose to forgive them, as well.

Now Lord, I choose to forgive all those who have ripped off my family in the past (list the oldest offenses in your family's history to the present, for example, the slave owners who ripped off your family's labor with no reparations).

Being ripped off, leave in Jesus' name.
Anger, leave.
Sin, leave.
Fear, leave.
Self-doubt, leave.
Depression, leave.
Pity, leave.
Lack of motivation, leave.
Hopelessness, leave.
Poor judgment, leave.
Inability to take risks, leave.
Inability to trust, leave.
Chaos, leave.
Instability, leave.
Blame, leave.
Gossip, leave.
Pessimism, leave.
Bitterness, leave.
Holding grudges, leave.

Optimism, return.
Love, return.
Trust, return.
Hope, return.
New opportunity, return.
Reparations, come.
Restitution, come.

Prosperity, return.
Gratitude, return.
Fortune, return.
Sharing, return.
Positive thinking, return.
Order, return.
Solidarity of family, return.
Letting go, return.
Moving on, return.
New beginnings, come.
Wisdom, return.
Discernment, return.
Forgiveness, return, and return, and return!

Lord, I release all those I've been holding prisoner in my mind, for their deeds done against my family, in Jesus' name.

Lord, if I have forgotten to forgive anyone else for cheating me or my family, please bring them to mind, so I can immediately forgive them, and move on.

I choose to no longer carry the burden of hating those who ripped us off.

I pray Lord for Your continuous protection and discernment, against being ripped off, for me, my children, and my children's children, for a thousand generations.

In Jesus' name. Amen.

42. THE BLAME GAME

Father, in the name of Jesus, I bring before You the curse of the blame game, and I ask that You would please remove it from my family line.

As a member of this family, I stand in the gap of my family line, and I cut, break, and sever all ties of the curse of the blame game off my family line.

I apologize for the family member who introduced this curse onto our family and I repent for their actions.

Please forgive them Lord, and all other family members who continually reintroduced this curse onto our line. Going all the way back to when Adam first blamed Eve for eating the forbidden fruit, to the beginning of our family line, and to this present day, I break off all involvement of this curse and I forgive all family members involved.

Lord I repent for all the times my family blamed others for their actions (list and forgive).
Lord I repent for all the times I blamed others for my actions (list and forgive).
Please forgive me Lord when I blamed people or events for my own mistakes in life, including when I blamed You.

Blame, leave.
Shame, leave.
Depression, leave.
Guilt, leave.
Self-doubt, leave.
Unfulfilled dreams, leave.
False pride, leave.
Fault finding in everything, leave.

Ownership of fault, return.
Forgiveness, return.
Hope, return.
Joy, return.
New ideas, return.
Humor, return.
Accomplishments, return.

Lord, I ask that You would please restore my family, to no longer hold the past, hostage. Show us who's at fault, grant us grace to forgive, and then please help us to move on.

Help us Lord, to stop blaming others. Help us to use our mistakes as lessons for growth, so that we can move on to bigger and better things. In Jesus' name. Amen.

43. BROKEN PROMISES and CAUGHT IN THE CROSSFIRE

Lord, in 1781, during the American Revolution, through British Proclamation, the British guaranteed freedom to over 5000 slaves, who fled their captors, only to end up serving the British army as free laborers. At the battle of Yorktown, Virginia, once British supplies ran low, in order to save their own soldiers, the British turned the slaves out into the open crossfire the British were having with the American and French armies. Those slaves that survived the storm of gunfire, would be forced to return to their masters.

Wow Lord, what does one say to that? If this has plagued my ancestors, Lord please remove from my family line, the curses of broken promises from our liberators, and then being caught in other people's crossfire. Lord, I apologize and repent for anyone in my family line (white or black) that participated in this curse. Please forgive their actions.

For anyone in my family line that was a victim of this atrocity and survived, Lord, please remove all physical and psychological damage from this, off my family line.

Lord, please grant us deliverance from our family members being caught between opposing enemies, when we've had nothing to do with their war. Please shield us from their bullets, both physically and mentally. Please shield us from being people's scapegoats, from being people's free labor, from being people's human shields in their crossfire. Lord, please take us to a place of refuge and peace, until they resolve their issues.

I choose to forgive anyone in my family line that initiated or perpetuated this curse. I break, cut, and sever all ties to the curses of broken promises from our liberators, and being caught in the crossfire of other peoples' battles, off me, off my children, and off my children's children for a thousand generations.

I choose to forgive the British for their broken promises to free my people, in order to promote their cause. I choose to forgive the British for exploiting my people to build and serve in their army camps. I choose to forgive the British for sending my people into the crossfire of no man's land, to be slaughtered like sheep, from both sides. And I choose to forgive the British for allowing the surviving slaves to be sent back to their slave masters.

Wow Lord, that's a lot to forgive. But I do it, choosing to turn over my will to You, to forgive, to be restored, and to move on! I pray all this, in the name of Jesus Christ, the One Who brutally suffered on a cross, for us. Amen!

www.britishbattles.com/battle-yorktown.htm
DVD: *Liberty! The American Revolution*, Director Ellen Hovde and Director Muffie Meyer

44. COMPLAINING

Lord, I can't keep my big mouth shut. Please forgive me for complaining all the time.

Father God, I know from the scriptures in the Old Testament (Numbers 11:1-3) that You hate complaining. It shows lack of faith in You, and it fuels the fires of despair.

So, in the name of Jesus, Lord I ask that You would please remove the curse of complaining off my family line.

I ask Lord that You would please forgive me, and my family members, both present and past from the sins of complaining.

I cut, break, and sever all ties to the curse of complaining off my family line.

I apologize and repent for the person who initiated this curse. If this curse was introduced by my ancestors who were slaves, I know You understand their grumblings, Lord. While I don't blame them Lord, I repent for their actions, and ask that You would forgive them for instilling a bitter root of complaining in our family line.

I bring before You Lord, various people in my family that are chronic complainers. Please forgive (list family folk and their complaints). I repent for their actions, and ask for Your forgiveness.

Lord, I ask that You would please remove all bitterness from my family tree. Please treat those bitter roots with Your restoration of forgiveness, contentment and gratitude.

I apologize for every time I complained about something, knowing things could be a lot worse.

I apologize for every time I engaged in other people's complaints, without sending back an encouraging word, or saying nothing at all.

Lord, help me to express what I'm feeling, without it turning into gossip.
Help me express what I'm feeling, without it turning into conversation that hurts You. Help me express my desires, without it turning into complaints about what I DON'T have.
Help me to check myself, when I'm complaining, but I'm actually jealous.
Help me to check myself, when I'm complaining, but I'm actually hurt.
Help me to check myself, when I'm complaining, but I'm actually mad at You, for not giving me what I want.

Forgive me Lord.

Forgive my family Lord.
Forgive my friends Lord, for fueling an unholy fire of complaints.

Complaining, leave.
Jealousy, leave.
Judgments, leave.
Gossip, leave.
Anger, leave.
Sadness, leave.
Powerlessness, leave.
Shame, leave.
Slander, leave.
Addiction to gossiping, leave.
Discontentment, leave.
Satan, leave.
Lying, leave.
Doubt, leave.
Believing lies, leave.
Envy, leave.
Blame, leave.
Victimization, leave.

I choose to forgive the people and situations in my life, that I complain about (list and forgive).

I choose to forgive myself, for not meeting my own expectations (list and forgive).

I forgive You Lord, for not giving me, what I want, when I want it.
Please forgive me Lord for hating on You.
Wow. Sorry for that.

Please forgive me for hating on others.

Contentment, return.
Fairness, return.
Edification (praising), return.
Joy, return.
Hope, return.
Love, return.
Good reports, return.
Good advice, return.
Good results, return.

When I see something's wrong, Lord, help me to pray about it, and shut up.

In Jesus' name. Amen.

45. THE COON

Father, in the name of Jesus, I ask that You would please break the curse of the coon, off everyone in my family line.

I cut, sever, and break all ties to the curse of the coon off me, my children, and my children's children, for a thousand generations.

I rebuke and renounce the stereotyped characteristics of the coon, like the character, Stepin Fetchit, off my race.

I rebuke all manners attributed to the coon as always having or being:
tall,
skinny,
lazy,
dark-skinned male,
head scratching
over-sized red lips,
dressed in rags,
dressed too showy,
slow moving,
having an exaggerated walk,
loose-jointed,
poor,
self-absorbed,
lacking ambition,
no skills for upward social mobility,
a buffoon,
frightened, bulging, darting eyes,
illiterate,
slurred speech,
embarrassing submissive replies, like "Yas suh, boss",
embarrassingly incompetent
historically funny to whites,
but dehumanizing for African-Americans.

I choose to forgive those in this nation that brought this negative stereotype onto the imagery of African-Americans, and I choose to forgive all the hurtful and harmful repercussions this stereotype had on blacks throughout its history in America.

Please remove this horrible image Lord Jesus, off our people.
Please restore the imagery of African-Americans, Lord, the way You originally intended…beautiful in Your sight!
In Jesus' name. Amen.

Dr. David Pilgrim, Professor of Sociology, Ferris State University
www.ferris.edu/jimcrow/caricature

46. CRABS IN A BARREL

The saying, "Blacks act like crabs in a barrel" is a curse.

Father, I ask that You would please remove the curse of crabs-in-a-barrel, off my family line and off this nation's consciousness.

I cut, break, and sever all ties to the curse of crabs-in-a-barrel, off me and my family's actions, in Jesus' name.

I ask that You would forgive the person who introduced this curse to our family line. I choose to forgive them as well.

If there was any carryover from my African ancestors, who were shoved and chained into slave ships as cargo, one on top of another, like crabs, then I break that abusive, physical, ancestral pattern, off my family line. I ask that You would forgive our captors, and I choose to forgive our captors, as well.

I ask Lord, that You would please forgive me, and anyone in my family that perpetuated this curse, by pulling fellow African-Americans down, in order to elevate ourselves.

Please forgive us every time we made ourselves superior over other blacks, intellectually, academically, economically, or socially.

Lord, I give You every time these incidences occurred, inside or outside of my family line (list, repent and forgive).

Lord, I choose to forgive every time my family members were made to feel inferior by other blacks (list and forgive). I give You Lord all the pain attached to these experiences.

Lord I choose to forgive every time I was made to feel inferior by other blacks (list and forgive). I give You Lord all my pain attached to these experiences.

No more tearing down one another Lord.
No more backbiting, Lord.
No more clawing, Lord.
No more being manipulated by white society to tear each other apart, Lord.

Help me lift up other blacks, Lord.
Help me build up other blacks, Lord.
Help me bring up other blacks, Lord, to new levels…..
…………………………..where there's plenty of room at the top, for us all.

In Jesus' name. Amen.

47. DEPRESSION

Father, in the name of Your Son, Jesus Christ, I come before You, asking You to please remove the curse of depression, off my family line.

I choose to forgive the person in my blood-line that introduced this curse onto our family, and I ask that You Lord would please forgive them.

In the name of Jesus, I cut, sever, and break all ties to the curse of depression off my family line.

I ask Lord that You would please heal me (if applies) and all my family members from every aspect of this emotion.

Please grant us the right medication (if needed) and the correct dosage.
Please grant us good counseling and a healthy community.
Please remove us from harmful circumstances that contribute to our depression.
Please remove all lies we may believe about ourselves or others.
Please remove all the hurt that continues to taunt us.
Please bring relief if we're still in mourning.
Please plant us in new places, where we may grow new perspectives.
Please grant us hope, in the areas where the enemy has destroyed our hope.
Please take away our comparisons with others, not feeling we measure up.
Please take away our unreasonable expectations of ourselves and others.
Please replace our unreasonable expectations with Your divine hope.
Please help us to make progress, step by step.
Please help us, in Your divine timing, to conquer our depression.

Steer us in the right direction, Lord.
Shed our doubt, Lord.
Restore our faith, Lord.
Revive us, Lord.

It is not Your will, that we live in darkness.
It is not Your will that we suffer needlessly, or bear undue sorrow.

Show us the way, out of this dark emotion, Lord Jesus. Please remove the veil from our eyes, granting Your light….that we might LIVE!

Depression, leave in the name of Jesus. Sorrow, leave in the name of Jesus. Lord, as a member of this family line, I give You all the generational depression of my family line and I ask You to please keep it off me, my children and my children's children, for a thousand generations.
Thank You Lord, for the miracle of JOY! Please bless us with a dose of Your JOY, everyday, Lord! In Jesus' name. Amen.

48. DISTRACTIONS

Father, in the name of Jesus, I ask that You would please remove the curse of distractions from my life.

Lord, there are things I need to get done, and I need Your help in doing them. But distractions just keep getting in my way.

Lord I cut, sever, and break, all ties to the curse of distractions off me, as well as my family's line.

Lord I apologize and repent for the actions of my family members who brought this curse onto our family line. I ask that You would please forgive them.

I choose to forgive whoever started this curse and all those in the family line that perpetuated this curse. I also choose to forgive myself (if applies) for participating in this curse, as well.

I ask for forgiveness Lord, for holding the current people or situations hostage in my heart. (List to God, anyone you're presently mad at, and forgive them, even if you don't feel like forgiving them. Then ask for forgiveness from God for being mad at them. This includes if you're mad at God for not giving you what you want.)

Anger toward God, leave. Anger toward myself, leave. Anger toward certain people, leave. Anger toward my circumstances, leave (call out each circumstance in your life that makes you mad, and command it to leave), in the name of Jesus. The fact that I keep finding things to distract me from doing my work, leave!

Distractions go, in Jesus' name. Hopelessness, leave. Sadness and depression, leave. Impatience, leave. Anger, leave. Irritability, leave. ADD, subside. ADHD, subside. Boredom, leave. Wasted time, leave. Cravings, leave. Busy work, leave. Self gratification without moderation, leave! People using me to do their work, leave. My inability to say, "No." to others, leave, in the name of Jesus!

Purpose, return. Confidence, return. Joy, return. Creativity, return. God's Energy, return. Good direction, return. Renewed strength, return. Discernment, return. Time management, return. Ability to say, "No." to distractions, return. Delayed gratification, return. Focus, return. Determination, return. Completing projects, return, in Jesus' name.

Lord, please keep the curse of distractions off me, my children, and my children's children for a thousand generations. In Jesus' name, I humbly ask You Lord to please help me follow through with that which You've called me to do, and receive the blessings of Your handy work, as well as my own.

In Jesus' name. Amen.

49. ENTERTAINMENT MEDIA'S RACIST STEREOTYPES

Father, in the name of Jesus, I ask that You would please remove the curse of the entertainment media's racist stereotypes, off every African-American in this country.

In the name of Jesus, I cut, break and sever all ties to the curse of racist stereotypes off every form of entertainment media, off me and my family line.

I ask that You would please forgive all whites that started this campaign of media exploitation centuries ago, and all those that perpetuated this curse, even to today.

I choose to forgive all those who initially inflicted this curse on my people, and all those who perpetuated the curse of racist stereotypes in every form of entertainment media, throughout American history.

I rebuke and renounce all media distortions of blacks, all poor or exaggerated physical descriptions of blacks, all un-even negative portrayals of black culture, and all negative stereotypes of black behavior.

I rebuke and renounce all hideous and hateful caricatures, which symbolized my people.

I forgive all actors, writers, producers, directors, composers, and artists that aided and abetted the negative imagery of blacks for profit, gain, status, or cruelty.

I forgive all negative imagery that caused (and still causes) racial prejudice and biased assumptions against my people.

I forgive all Coon characters (tall, skinny, loose-jointed, poor, dark skinned oafs)
I forgive all Brute characters (angry, strong, animalistic, violent black males)
I forgive all Uncle Tom characters (kind servants to whites, intellectually childlike)
I forgive all Mammy characters (sassy, overweight servants, loyal to white families)
I forgive all Picaninny characters (black babies)
I forgive all Sapphire characters (angry black women)
I forgive all Jezebel characters (black women as sex objects)
I forgive all Tragic Mulatto characters (sad people from black and white parents)

I rebuke and renounce all these negative images off my race, in the name of Jesus.

We want it all gone, Lord.
Please make these racist stereotypes in the media obsolete in our American culture. Please replace the entertainment media's social, economic, and political discrimination of African-Americans, with positive, fair, and balanced representation, from this time, forth. In Jesus' name. AMEN!

Dr. David Pilgrim, Professor of Sociology, Ferris State University
www.ferris.edu/jimcrow/caricature/

50. ENTITLEMENT TO OVER-EAT

Father, in the name of Jesus, I ask that You would please remove the curse of entitlement to over-eat, off my family line.

What I mean by this Lord is, I'm asking You to please forgive those in my family, that used the right to eat (whatever they wanted, whenever they wanted), as a reward system for personally sacrificing themselves for someone else, or something else.

For instance, when family members sacrificed their dreams, to become caregivers for a loved one OR sacrificed their goals to fulfill someone else's goals OR sacrificed their freedom in place of someone else's freedom; these and other examples where family members gave up their own ambitions to serve someone else, they then used eating food as a means to comfort and compensate themselves, to deal with their self-sacrifice.

I ask You Lord to please break this pattern of entitlement to over-eat off my family line. Because in some situations Lord, where there is no comfort, family members are eating themselves to death.

I cut, break and sever all ties to the curse of entitlement to over-eat off my family line. Lord, I don't know who introduced this curse to my family line. I'm sure a lot of entitlement eating occurred during slavery when my family members had no power, especially over their family members being sold or beaten. I can see how food became a reward system.

I choose not only to forgive that family member for introducing this curse to the family line, but I empathize with them Lord. I choose to forgive everyone responsible, inside and outside our family line, for perpetuating this horrible habit in our family.

I apologize for all, including myself (if applies) who have engaged in this curse, and ask Lord that You would please reverse the effects of using food as a reward.

Lord I give You all those in my family line who were overweight and who sacrificed their lives for someone else (list all, forgiving them and the people or circumstances they sacrificed for). I choose to forgive them for entitlement eating.

Lord, I give You the family members who are currently overweight, who are sacrificing their lives for others, right now (list all, forgiving them and the people or circumstances causing them to over-eat). I choose to forgive them and myself (if applies) for entitlement eating.

I break the curse of entitlement eating off each and every one of us, in Jesus' holy name.

Entitlement to over-eat, leave.
The false empowerment eating gives us, leave in Jesus' name.
Justification to over-eat, leave.
Poor eating habits, leave.
Food addictions, leave.
Dependence on endorphins through food, leave.
Dependence on dopamine through food, leave.
Excuses, leave.
Anger from self-sacrificing, leave.
Anger toward others, leave.
Blame, leave.
Sadness, leave.
Self-pity, leave.
Chemical dependence, leave.
Love of eating whenever I want, leave.
Obsession with food, leave.
Boredom eating, leave.
Emotional eating, leave.
Powerlessness, leave.
Feeling unloved, leave.
Fear, leave.
Feeling like a failure, leave in Jesus' name.

Empowerment through Christ, come.
Support systems through community, return.
Relief from self-sacrificing, come quickly.
Ability to live out personal dreams, return.
Achieving personal goals, return.
Time for one's self, return.
Restoration, return.
Entitlement to one's own life, return.
Only eating when hungry, return.
Satisfaction with small portions, return.
Self-satisfaction, return.
Joy, return.
Endorphins, through healthy relationships, return.
Dopamine, through healthy relationships, return.
Healthy outlets, return.

Lord, please keep this curse away from my family, from me, my children, and my children's children, for a thousand generations.
In Jesus' name. Amen

www.webmd.com/diet/features/compulsive-overeating-and-how-to-stop-it

51. EXCESSIVENESS

Like the Egyptian kings and queens of Africa, Lord, I recognize the desire to have a pyramid full of stuff. But seeing that we can't take it with us, when we leave this earth, I ask Lord that You would please help me control my accumulation of stuff, by removing the curse of excessiveness, off my family line.

I come before You, understanding that when my family members were kidnapped from Africa, they were stripped of everything. This may have left my family line, wanting.

Father, in the name of Jesus, I break and sever all ties to the curse of excessiveness off me and everyone in my family line. I break the curse of idolizing "stuff".

I burn the roots of this curse where my ancestors were kidnapped and stripped of everything, including their heritage, their identity, and their freedom. I burn the roots of this curse at the points of slavery, where my ancestors had little possessions.

I choose to forgive all abductors and slave masters who hindered my ancestors from having anything of their own, including freedom for themselves or their loved ones.

I choose to forgive those in my family line that habitually accumulated things, in order to feel powerful, especially in a society that continually tries to take our power away.

I choose to forgive those in my family line that over-consume, due to their insecurities, and I forgive those that burdened our family with debt, due to their need for excess.

I ask that You would forgive us all, Lord, and restore our balance of need and want, to our family line, to me, my children, and my children's children, for a thousand generations and help us NOT to buy into the world's definition of excess, as being successful.

Help my family to focus on what is important in life (You, family, friends, community, health, worship) to live the long life You have planned for us.

Help us not to take pride in our possessions, but joy in what You've freely given us. Please break the curse of needing stuff, in order to validate our being.

Also Lord, help us to take care of what You've given us. Not just looking at everything as being disposable.

Lord, please teach me how to appreciate what I have, and to share it, whenever possible. In Jesus' name. Amen!

52. EXPLOSIVE ANGER

Father, in the name of Jesus, I ask that the curse of explosive anger be removed from my family line. Please forgive us.

As a member of this family, I stand before You Lord, asking that You would first forgive me for all the times I've had explosive anger. I repent to You and apologize for losing my temper. I'm sorry for (list every time you flew off the handle and apologize to God). I choose to forgive myself for my behavior, and I pray for help to get my explosive anger under Your control.

I choose to forgive everyone that ever went off on me. (Name every incident someone screamed at you and forgive them. Remember, you don't have to "feel" like forgiving them, you're turning your will over to Christ, by "choosing" to forgive them.)

Lord, whether my temper comes from stress, environmental pressures, financial worries, post traumatic stress, genetic traits, family problems, a misunderstanding of what's going on, not enough support, frustration at my job, or just being tired, Lord, I give these all to You.

As a member of this family, I cut, break, and sever all ties to the curse of explosive anger and remove it from our family line.

I choose to forgive the family member that brought this curse on our family. I also apologize for all my family members that acted out in violent anger, before You Lord. I repent and I apologize to You Lord, for what they did, and what the repercussion of their anger did, to our family line. Lord, as a member of this family, I stand in the gap, asking for Your forgiveness for our explosive anger, in the name of Jesus of Nazareth, the Lamb of God, Who shed His blood on the cross for the remission of our sins.

Lord, I give You our explosive anger. Lord, I give You the lies, that say, "If we don't keep our rage, we are helpless. We are weak. We are insignificant."

Lord, please, take away whatever it is that makes us lose our temper.
Please give us what we need to change, for me, my family, my children, and my children's children, for a thousand generations.

If we need counseling, grant us that, Lord.
If we need money, grant us that, Lord.
If we need someone to help us, grant us that Lord.
If we need a rest, grant us that Lord.
If we need to get away from the people we're around, grant us that, Lord.
If we need to rely on You for all our needs, You've already granted us that, Lord.
In Jesus' name. Amen.

53. FAT GENE

God, is there such a thing as a fat gene? If so, does my family have it?
When I look at family members and old family photos, I see a pattern Lord.
I see obesity.

So, Father, in the name of Jesus, I ask that You would please remove the curse of the fat gene from my family's molecular structure.

I cut, break, and sever all ties to the curse of the fat gene, and while I'm at it, the cancer gene, the alcoholic gene, and any other bad genes embedded in my family line.

I apologize on behalf of the family member that introduced this curse to our line. I ask that You would please forgive them, Lord. If this condition truly is a predisposition for weight gain, then I ask that You'd change it, in Jesus' name. Please restore my family line Lord, to Your original concept of healthy people.

I give You Lord, all our shame of being obese, in Jesus' name. I give You Lord, all the needless deaths that occurred because of this condition. If I am harboring any anger or frustration toward You Lord, for allowing this genetic condition in my family line, then I choose to forgive You Lord, and I ask for forgiveness for my anger toward You.

Fat gene, leave in Jesus' name. Anger, leave. Self-hate, leave. Doubt, leave. Shame, leave. Fear, leave. Self-consciousness, leave. Ignorance to my condition, leave. Self-defeat, leave, in Jesus' name.

If there are ways my family can counter our obesity, please show us the way, Lord.

If my family eliminated daily exercise from their lives, due to 200 years of "free" exercise being slaves, please show us how to exercise, where it doesn't feel laborious.
If stress is a huge contributor to our obesity, Lord, please reduce the stress in our lives.
If the once healthy African diet of our ancestors, has been replaced by a poor American diet, Lord, please reintroduce to us, the habit of eating the best foods for our genetic constitution….and let it taste good, Lord.

Destroy in us, the addiction to the foods that are killing us. Please reset our bodies biologically, Lord, stopping the invisible things that cause us to eat. Please bring us back into harmony, balancing our emotions, our hormones and anything else that drive us to eat, beyond our hunger. Please eliminate the fat gene from our family line, Lord, that we may live long, healthy and fruitful lives, from me, from my children, and from my children's children, for a thousand generations. In Jesus' name. Amen

54. FEAR OF FAILURE

Father God, in the name of Jesus, I come before Your throne, asking that You would please remove the curse of the fear of failure off my life, and my family's generational line.

I cut, sever, and break, all ties to the curse of the fear of failure off me and my family line. I ask Lord if You would please forgive the family member who originally introduced this curse onto our family line. I choose to forgive them and all in my family, that perpetuated this curse. I also choose to forgive all those outside our family, that throughout history, killed the dreams of our family members. In the name of Jesus, I cancel all dream killers, attached to my family's line.

Lord, this curse immobilizes us, from getting anything done for fear we won't succeed. I can't seem to get motivated to start or finish, anything.

Lord I choose to forgive myself, my family, friends, teachers, and anyone else I've looked up to in the past, that put down my aspirations, laughed at my ideas, caused me to fail, dissuaded me from pursuing my dreams, or actually stopped me from following my goals. I choose to forgive You Lord, for not helping me to fulfill my dreams as well. Please forgive me for harboring any anger toward You, Lord.

I take full responsibility for not completing my dreams, goals, and commitments. I bring every incompletion in my life before You Lord, and I choose to forgive them (list every failure, starting from your childhood and forgive everyone involved, including yourself).

Lord I choose to give You all my sadness in my failures. Lord I give You the weight of my failures that I have been carrying on my shoulders. Fear of failure, leave. Sadness, leave. Guilt, leave. Shame, leave. Lack of motivation, leave. Lack of confidence, leave. Doubt, leave. Excuses, leave. Competition with others, leave. False pride, leave. Jealousy, leave. Discouragement from others, leave. Naiveté, leave. Laziness, leave. Procrastination, leave in the name of Jesus.

Lord, I come before You, asking You to direct me. Help me to use my strengths and accept my weaknesses. Help me to stop procrastinating and start focusing. Please Lord, help me to dig in to what You would have me to do and bring it into completion.

Lord, I choose to trust You for my success. Lord, please remind me of all the times I did accomplish my goals (list and thank God and congratulate yourself). Thank You Lord, for being the strength of my life. Help me to move forward with You, into the next phase of what You have in store for my life and my family's life. In Jesus' name. Amen!

55. FEELING LIKE YOU NEVER PLEASE YOUR PARENTS

Father, in the name of Jesus, I give to You the curse of feeling like we never please our parents, and I humbly ask that You would please remove it from our family line.

Lord, I cut, sever and break all ties to the curse of feeling like we never please our parents, off me and my family line.

Lord, I ask that You would please forgive the person who introduced this curse to my family line, and I choose to forgive them also. I cut, sever and break off the complicated expectations that were passed down from our slave ancestors, who set up survival tactics for their children not to be sold, whipped or killed, in order to maintain their family's preservations on the plantation. I break off any existing slave mentality off our family line, which once kept us alive, but now is obsolete. I break off all slave instructions that were mandated throughout our family line for our own protection. I break off all slave/post Civil War/Jim Crow instructions that insisted we stay in our place.

I reclaim the freedom that my family members legally received, and I thank You Lord that we may claim every aspect of our legal and divine right to be free.

I pray that You would forgive those family members, even with the best intentions, for hurting their children with their excessive disapproval. I break off all psychological holds parents put on their children, by their excessive disapproval. I break off all judgments, criticisms, jokes, blame, guilt, manipulations, physical and/or verbal abuse, done by family members. I choose to forgive all their actions.

Feeling like I never please my parents, leave in Jesus' name. Self-blaming, leave. Anger, leave. Shame, leave. Never measuring up, leave. Self-medicating, leave.

I choose to forgive my own parents (list whatever they said or did to make you feel like you didn't please them and forgive them).

I ask (if applies) Lord that You would forgive me for leading my children to believe I'm not pleased with them (list every time you did this, ask them for forgiveness, then forgive yourself).

Lord, please restore to our family line, positive feelings toward our parents and our children. May we always let our children know that we are well pleased with them. May our parents let us know, they are well pleased with us. May the criticism stop. May the healing begin.

If it is impossible for us to receive approval from our parents, grant us ample grace to forgive our parents. Please Lord, fill us with the knowledge, that You are our true parent, and that Your love for us, is unconditional. In Jesus' name. Amen.

56. FINANCES BEING MISHANDLED

Father, in the name of Jesus, I ask that You would remove the curse of finances being mishandled, off my family line.

Lord I repent and apologize for anyone in my family line that brought and perpetuated this curse in our family line. I ask that You would please forgive them and their actions.

I cut, break, and sever all ties to the curse of finances being mishandled off my family line, in the name of Jesus.

I choose to forgive all those members in my family line (black and white) that abused, stole, or squandered or illegally invested the family finances (list and forgive).

Please forgive me (if applies) for mishandling the family's finances (list, repent saying you're sorry to God, then forgive yourself). I ask for forgiveness Lord, for every time I did this, and I choose to forgive myself for my actions.

I humbly ask Lord, that You would please restore our finances. I ask Lord that You would please restore everything that was stolen, given away, or lost in our family line.

In Jesus' name. Amen.

57. FOOD

Father, in the name of Jesus, would You please remove the curse of abusing food, off my family line.

I cut, break and sever all ties to the curse of abusing food, off my family line.

I ask Lord, that You would please forgive anyone in my family line that brought on this curse. Also, please forgive the people who provoked the circumstances around this curse.

I choose to forgive all overseers and masters that took away the rights of my family to grow, cook and eat what was native to their diets in Africa.

I choose to forgive all foods that were introduced to us that would prove to be harmful to our life expectancy.

Lord please remove from our family line, the desires for those foods that are harmful to our bodies, yet delicious to our pallets.

If starvation was a root cause for my family hoarding food, I cancel the roots of starvation off my family line. I choose to forgive all government officials, law-makers, policing authorities, landowners, bureaucrats, and slave masters, who withheld food from my ancestors. I choose to forgive all those who participated in the starvation of my ancestors.

I ask Lord that You would please forgive anyone in my family who cursed people who withheld food from them or stole food from them, even if it was by the orders of their slave masters or cruel task masters.

I plead the blood of Jesus over every situation where my family members starved or caused others to starve and I ask that you would release us from this curse, in Jesus' name.

Lord, I give You my lust for food. I look back on my family line and I can say I know people in my family line who have used food as a crutch. So I ask that You would please remove the curse of dependency on food as a crutch, off my family line.

Lord I cancel all dependency on food which my family line uses for comfort. I cancel using food to comfort us as a coping mechanism to deal with the harsh things in our lives. Lord I ask that You would forgive me, and everyone in my family line that uses food as a crutch, instead of turning to You to help us resolve the issues in our lives.

I choose to forgive my parents for teaching me bad eating habits. I choose to forgive all psychological damage they planted in training me to over-eat. Lord please cut all poor diets given to me as a child, or being made to eat everything on my plate. I cut the tie of force feeding and being made to feel guilty for not eating all my food. Lord I give You the guilt of over-eating.

Lord please sever from me all ties to emotionally eating. Show me when I'm being triggered, and help me to immediately give You every bad emotion, when they occur.

I also give You the generational fear of never having enough to eat. I cut, break and sever all ties to being fat as a status symbol of prosperity.

I also cut, break and sever all ties to being fat as a means of protection from those who may harm me, using it as a camouflage from being attractive to harmful people.

Please be my Protector Lord from all harm, especially when I'm in the midst of wolves.
Please grant me discernment on how to stay away, or get out of scary situations. If I have been hurt in the past, grant me the courage to speak out when I am being harmed, and please see to it Lord that I receive full justice or retribution for my assault.

I ask that You'd forgive me, when I over-eat, and I choose to forgive myself for every time I over-eat.

I pray that You would restore to me and my family line, healthy foods.
Lord, would You teach us how to eat in moderation.

I ask that You'd free me, from what drives me to eat, Lord.
I ask that You'd take that person or situation away, in Jesus' name.
I choose to forgive every person or situation that drives me to eat.

Lord, I choose to give You my grief, my sadness, my lack of control,
my inability to deal with my current situation, my abusive past,
my neglected past, all feelings of inadequacy, and anything and everything that makes me over-eat.

I choose to go to You as my Comfort and Shield.

Please help me to unlock the reasons I gorge myself, and give every reason to You.

In the name of the Father, the Son and the Holy Ghost. In Jesus' name. Amen

58. HATERS

Father, in the name of Jesus, I ask that You would please forgive all the haters in my life.

I choose to forgive every person I have come across in my lifetime, who hated me, with or without probable cause. I stand in my generational line, and I choose to forgive every person who hated my family line or persecuted my family line because of their hatred.

I give You Lord, all the centuries of pain my family line endured by haters.

Today, I choose to forgive all white people (seen and unseen) who hate us.
Today, I choose to forgive all black people (seen and unseen) who hate us.

In the name of Jesus Christ of Nazareth, I cancel, cut and break all ties to the curse of haters off me and my family line.

I cancel all the power given to hatred, which has existed in my family line. I apologize on behalf of my family. If I or any member of my family members, brought on this curse by sinning against You Lord or some person(s), please forgive us Lord, and please dismiss all our hatred, by the blood of the Lamb.

I now list, and choose to forgive all those I know who have hated me and my family. Please bring to mind Lord, anyone I fail to mention that I need to forgive and let go.

We know that as long as sin is in the world, hate will exist. We also know that people, who hate others, actually hate themselves.

But Lord, by Your Blood and forgiveness, I choose to turn my will over to You:
to not allow hate to control me
to not allow hate to define me
to not allow hate to change my destiny
to not allow hate to keep me from every blessing You have for me.

Lord, I choose _not_ to let the enemy of my soul destroy me.
I choose to LOVE.
I choose to be guided by Your Spirit.
I choose to not allow haters, to hurt me anymore.
Praises to You Lord, the living God, Who Is LOVE!
Please fill me with Your Spirit Lord, consuming all hatred from around me, against me, and in me. Fill me with Your Love Lord, which surpasses all understanding!
In Jesus' name. Amen.

DVD: *Katt Williams, American Hustle,* Director Brit McAdams (inappropriate for children)

59. HIDDEN AGENDAS

Father, in the name of Jesus, I pray Thee to please remove the curse of being fooled by people's hidden agendas.

I cut, break, and sever all ties to the curse of being manipulated by people's hidden agendas. I pray that You would please reveal all hidden agendas to me Lord, in the name of the Father, and the Son, and the Holy Spirit.

Lord, I choose to forgive the family member(s) that initiated this curse onto our family line. I choose to forgive my slave family members, for any misdeeds they had to do, in order to survive. But maybe as time went by, my family's survival skills took on a form of manipulation that offended You. If so, I repent for my family's actions, and I ask that You would please forgive them and myself for any time our hidden agendas offended You.

I choose to forgive all those in my family line, who have used hidden agendas to hurt others (list any family you know of, what they did, and forgive them).

I choose to forgive all those in the past, who have had hidden agendas against me or my family (list any people you know of, what they did, and forgive them).

Hidden agendas, leave. Manipulation, leave. Naiveté, leave. Anger, leave. Victimization, leave. Sadness, leave. Depression, leave. Veil over my eyes, leave. Deafness to what people are really saying, leave. Guile, leave. Division, leave. Exclusion, leave. False hope, leave. Reliance on the wrong leaders, leave. Gossip, leave. Poor information, leave. Laziness not to check the facts, leave. False hope, leave. The haunting of past failures, leave. Fear of failure, leave. Fear, leave. Apathy, leave in Jesus' name.

Agendas revealed, return. Discernment, return. Openness, return. Courage to confront other's agendas, return. Fairness, return. Ability to change bad agendas, return. Openness to what the Holy Spirit is saying, return. Joy, return. Options, return. Opportunity, return. Trust in one's own gut, return. Awareness of people's lies, return. Trust in one's own experience, return. Trust in God, return! Hope, return. Love, return. New outlook, return. Fervently seeking the truth, return. God's opportunities to have the truth revealed, return. Progress, return. God's best, return.

Lord, You are the Truth and the Light. I love You.
I pray You will protect me, my children, and my children's children for a thousand generations, from people's hidden agendas.
I pray You will make all agendas apparent to us, in the name of the Father and the Son and the Holy Spirit.
Please grant my generational line, the gift of discernment. In Jesus' holy name. Amen.

60. HUMILIATION OF BEING UNEMPLOYED or RETIRED

Father God, it can be humiliating being unemployed. It can also be humiliating being retired. If our identity is wrapped up in "who we are" by "what we do", and we don't have a job, or are doing "nothing", then we feel like nothing.

This is not true. This is a lie from the pit of hell.

So, in the name of Jesus, I cut, sever and break off every tie to the curse of feeling humiliated for being unemployed or retired, off my family line.

For years, my family line worked for free, enslaved in this nation. This is not an excuse, but I pray for an understanding that when a person is forced to work against their will, a bitterness can develop, as well as a psychosis, that if they are not working, they are not worthy.

Lord, I ask that You would please break all slave mentality about work, off my family line. Lord, I ask that You would break off any twisted or unhealthy thoughts, or curses about being employed or unemployed.

Please break off all curses of bad employment off our family line, where there's a history of our family being abused, humiliated, or breaking the law, in order to make a living.

I give You Lord the crushing emotion of humiliation of not being employed or retired.

Humiliation, leave in the name of Jesus. Especially in the unemployment offices.

I choose to forgive all those, who have made me feel bad for not having a job, whether intentional or unintentional (List family, friends, and institutions. Forgive them all).

Humiliation of being unemployed or retired, leave in the name of Jesus.
Shame, leave.
Worthlessness, leave.
Jealousy, leave.
Rivalry, leave.
Excuses, leave.
Desperateness, leave.
Anxiety, leave.
Blame, leave.
Anger, leave.
Bitterness, leave.
Gossip, leave.
All grudges, leave.

If someone owes me anything from my old job, I choose to forgive them and let them go.
If someone wronged me from my old job, I choose to forgive them and let them go.

Father God, during slavery, blacks were put in "nigger jails" (holding cells) in America, where they'd wait for months to be sold off by their owners or the banks. If any of my family members suffered the humiliation of that ordeal, I choose to forgive those who were responsible.

If there was anyone in my family line, who as a slave was sold off, <u>not</u> for doing a poor job, but for their owner's financial gain, I come before You Jesus, and I break off the guilt, the confusion, the grief and the humiliation my ancestors felt being sold, with no power to change their relocation or their freedom.

Generational guilt and shame, leave.
Generational confusion, leave.
Generational grief, leave.
Generational humiliation, leave.
Generational powerlessness, leave.
Generational relocation against our wills, leave.
Generational being taken advantage of, leave.
Generational lack of freedom, leave.
Generational anger, leave.
Generational despondence, leave.
Generational blame, leave.
Generational jealousy, leave.
Generational unfair wages, leave.
Generational lack of motivation, leave.
Generational lack of promotions, leave.
Generational laziness, leave.
Generational bad advice, leave.
Generational bad leadership, leave.
Generational not being heard at work, leave.
Generational poor performance at work, leave.
Generational drama at work, leave.

Please put us in a place of rejuvenation Lord.
Please put us in a place where we can grow, and not be stagnant, Lord.
Please put us in a place where we're of good service, Lord.
Please put us in a place where we can contribute and be heard, Lord.
Please put us in a place where our gifts and talents soar, Lord.
Please put us in a place, that glorifies You, Lord.
I pray this, not only for us, but for our children, and our children's children, for a thousand generations. In Jesus' name. Amen. And Amen

Charleston's Walking Slave Tour – Fall 2012

61. INACCESSIBILITY TO ACCESS CODES

Heavenly Father, through Your Son Jesus Christ, thank You for access to You, the Author of Creation.

Lord, in the name of Jesus, please remove the curse of inaccessibility to access codes that would benefit us, off my family line. Please remove the barriers that keep us from information and inclusion.

Lord, in the name of Jesus, I break the curse of inaccessibility to access codes off my family line. I break, cut, and sever all curses that keep me and my family out of areas where we wish to belong and thrive.

Lord, from the time this nation was founded, coming from the classist society of Great Britain, the root curse of exclusion was established in our nation. As a citizen of this country, I break off all the root curses of exclusion that continued after the Revolutionary war, throughout slavery, the Civil War, Reconstruction, throughout the 20th century, and on to today. I break off the established exclusion in our country, where no matter how high up we rise, we are still denied <u>complete</u> access to all levels of American society.

Lord I come to You in the name of Jesus Christ, and by the blood of the Lamb, I breakthrough the invisible ceilings that have been placed before me, be they informational, economical, educational, social, spiritual, intellectual, inspirational, physical, personal or in the work place.

I ask for forgiveness for anyone in my blood line (black or white) that unfairly excluded people, and I choose to forgive any one in my family line that excluded or denied people access. I choose to forgive anyone who has denied me or my family, complete access to things (list and forgive).

I want to be careful here, Lord. I wish to give You any animosity (anger) I have toward people or organizations that have denied me access to anything in the past. I choose to give You Lord Jesus, any unnecessary desires I have to access things I don't need or are harmful. Help me understand, that in the climb to have greater access and the need to acquire more access codes, there can be an unhealthy seduction. Lead me not, into temptation, but delivery me from evil, Lord.

If obtaining access codes, will be a help to me and my family, and not a hindrance, then I ask for Your favor, Lord. Please Lord, may the doors of exclusion be opened, so that my family and my heirs may have their fair share.

Please restore what was robbed or taken in the past from our family line, that we may be blessed and be a blessing to others in the future. This I pray for me, my children, and my children's children for a thousand generations. In Jesus' name. Amen.

62. INJURIES and NEAR DEATH EXPERIENCES WITH KIDS

Lord, I've noticed this pattern with children in my family. So Father, in the name of Jesus, I ask You to please remove the curse of injuries and near death experiences with children, off my family line.

I cut, break and sever the curse of injuries and near death experiences with children, off my family line, by the Blood of the Lamb, Jesus Christ of Nazareth, off me, off my children, and off my children's children, for a thousand generations.

Father, please forgive the person who brought this curse of child injuries, near fatal accidents, and children's deaths on our family line. I repent for their actions, in the name of Jesus of Nazareth. I choose to forgive this person (white or black), and I ask You to please forgive the actions of all those who contributed to this curse.

I choose to forgive all those outside my family line, who hurt, harmed, or killed the children in my family line throughout this country's history. In the name of Jesus, I choose to forgive the brutalization of stealing children in my family from Africa, the selling of our children into slavery, and any other atrocities that I don't know about where children in my family line were harmed or killed.

I choose to forgive the white side of my family line that participated in the brutalization of harming, hurting, or murdering children. I repent, Lord Jesus, for all their actions, and I ask Lord, that You would please forgive them for everything they did. (List any events you know where your family members were guilty of harming or killing children, apologize to God for their actions, then you forgive them.)

Injuries and near death experiences with children, leave in Jesus' name. Sorrow, leave. Powerlessness, leave. Anger, leave. Confusion, leave. Shame, leave.

I choose to forgive those in my family, that allowed me to be injured as a child (forgive all injuries and near death experiences that happened to you as a child, including forgiving your mom and dad for their lack of supervision, and God for not fully protecting you--don't worry, He can handle it).

I choose to forgive myself (if applies) for allowing my children to be injured. (List every major injury your children experienced, near death or death. Be sure to forgive all those involved, and yourself, even if it wasn't your fault. Forgive God for not protecting your children. You may be holding a grudge against God-don't worry, He can handle it.)

I thank You Lord, for preserving our family, thus far, never leaving us or forsaking us. Please continue Your protection over our family line. In Jesus' name. Amen.

63. JEALOUSY

Father, in the name of Jesus, I ask that You would please remove the curse of jealousy from my family line.

As a member of this family, I cut, break and sever all ties to the curse of jealousy off my family line.

I choose to forgive the family member that introduced this curse onto our family, and I forgive everyone in my family line that continues to reinstate this curse, generationally.

I ask Lord that You would forgive all of us in the family line, who participated in this curse, and I apologize for all our actions.

In the times I've witnessed jealousy in my family (and friends), I bring each incident before You Lord, and I choose to forgive each person involved (list every time people were jealous of you, forgive them all, even if their jealousy doesn't make sense to you).

Lord, now I ask You to please forgive me, for every time I was jealous of others (list every time you were jealous of people, even when you were a child, apologize to God, ask for forgiveness, then forgive yourself).

Lord, please sever all cords of jealousy that have made me and my family line, bitter.

I ask Lord that jealous comments, no longer have power over me or my family members.

Jealousy, leave.
Bitterness, leave.
Comparisons, leave.
Competitiveness, leave.
Coveting, leave.
The grass is always greener, leave.
Discontentment, leave.
Unmet dreams, leave.
Broken promises, leave.
Failed expectations, leave.
Awkwardness, leave.
Hopelessness, leave.
Back biting, leave.
Belittling everyone and everything, leave.
Critical spirit, leave.
Gossip, leave.

Trying to please people who can never be pleased, leave.
Doubt, leave.
Self-doubt, leave.
Depression, leave.
Anger, leave.
Lack of motivation, leave.
Shutting people down, leave.
Lies, leave!
False hope, leave.
Needing to be liked by everyone, leave.
Silliness, leave.
Holding on to criticisms from the past, leave!
Ungratefulness, leave!
Living an unfulfilled life, leave.
Condemnation leave.
Judgment leave, in the name of Jesus.

Please Lord remove the veil of jealousy from our eyes, that blinds us from seeing people the way You see people.

Forgiveness, return.
Grace, return.
Being happy for others, return.
New dreams, return.
New goals, return.
New plans, return.
Help to execute those plans, return.
Mentoring, return.
Fulfilled dreams, return.
God's Love for myself, return.
God's Love for others, return.
Bridge building, return.
Peace, return.
Joy for others, return.
Praise for others, return.
Appreciation for others, return.
Gratitude, return.
Contentment, return.

These blessings I ask Lord, for my family line, for me, for my children, and for my children's children, for a thousand generations.

In Jesus' name. Amen.

64. JIM CROW

(This prayer may not apply to you. But it's good to pray for other black families in this nation. Not all our people walked away from Jim Crow, unscathed.)

Father, in the name of Jesus, I come before You, standing as a representative of my family line.

I choose to forgive all those who initiated, created, wrote, edited, promoted, produced,
published,
ratified,
voted,
lobbied,
blackmailed,
terrorized,
dehumanized,
politicized,
mimicked,
compromised,
scapegoated,
legislated laws, bylaws, rules and regulations that limited and eliminated African-American power in this country.

I forgive every United States President, Congressman, Senator, Supreme Court Judge, legislator, attorney, business proprietor, realtor, banker, sheriff, capitalist, investor, corporate financier, public servant; teacher, preacher, physician, civil engineer, historian, scientist and any other persons with authority and influence in this nation, who sided with these laws of segregation, humiliation, and discrimination against my family and blacks through this country's history.

I ask Lord that You would forgive all these people for participating in Jim Crow and I ask Lord that You would release the curse of Jim Crow off our nation, our states, our cities, our counties, our suburbs, and all our rural regions.

I ask Lord that if anyone in my family (black or white), contributed to bringing this curse onto our family line, that You would forgive them, and I choose to forgive them for not honoring You.

I ask that You Lord, would please remove all effects that were laid upon my family and any other African-American family, from the curse of Jim Crow.

I ask that You Lord, would please restore, all that the enemy took from us.
Please restore our full rights as US citizens to live freely in this democracy.
Please Lord restore our rights as black citizens to vote.
Please restore our rights to live wherever we can afford.

Please restore our rights to receive a free and excellent public education.
Please restore our rights to drive wherever we want without being harassed.
To use the restroom where we want,
To drink from any faucet we want.
To eat wherever we want, without feeling threatened.
To vote for whom we want.
To socialize freely (and orderly) in a public area, without being discriminated against.
To be transported freely, without discrimination.
To serve in the military, and be promoted the way we want.
To speak where we want.
To receive top medical attention when we want.
To learn and have access to higher education, where we want.
To work where we want.
To be promoted fairly, when and where we want.
To be paid a fair wage, when we work.
To play where we want.
To shop where we want.
To vacation where we want.
To be celebrated where we want.
To build, grow and expand where we want.
To contribute to the good of society how we want.
To worship You, whenever, however, and wherever we want.

Lord, please cut, cancel, and abolish all color lines in this country, visible and invisible. Please tear up all "separate but equal" institutions from their very foundations. I call on You Lord Jesus to please uproot the beginning of the practice of slavery, which was established in Jamestown Virginia in 1619.

Though African slaves and European indentured servants built this nation side by side, I cancel, in the name of Jesus, the turning point to a color code set in 1640 by Virginia's highest court, who first mandated (in the case of John Punch serving a lifetime sentence for running away, compared to his two white counterparts who only served extra time) that blacks' rights, would legally be considered inferior to whites. I cancel this beginning of the Jim Crow society.

I choose to forgive the initial racist sentencing of John Punch, and I ask You Lord to please forgive the Virginia courts for this judgment, as well. I ask that You Lord would please remove every act of Jim Crow from that time, to this very day, off me, my family line, and off every other African-American family in this country.

Please free us from this tyranny Lord. Please set the laws straight in this nation, Lord. In the name of the Father, and the Son, and the Holy Ghost. Amen.

Dr. David Pilgrim, Professor of Sociology, **Ferris State University**
http://www.ferris.edu/jimcrow/menu.htm
http://en.wikipedia.org/wiki/Jim_Crow_laws
DVD: *Slavery in America,* Director Dante J. James, Director Gail Pellett, Director Chana Gazit, and Director Leslie D. Farrell

65. LACK OF OPPORTUNITY FOR OUR BLACK YOUTH

Father, in the name of Your Son Jesus, I humbly ask that You would please lift off the curse of the lack of opportunity, for today's black youth.

Historically, this country has done everything in its power to disengage and disenfranchise our black youth. From poor and segregated schools, to drug infested communities, to generational imprisonment and recidivism, it's a wonder how our young people have survived. Lord, please forgive this nation and its history for establishing and perpetuating this curse on our black youth.

We come before Your throne, asking You to please correct our nation's history, by providing endless positive opportunities for our black youth in this country. Please Lord, help our young people to develop, thrive and excel in programs, jobs, loving homes, safe environments, good schools and great learning programs that will not only match their style of learning, but help them excel in their talents. Please Lord, grant us positive programs that will not only enhance our black youth's talents, but will allow our black youths to celebrate and share their gifts with the world.

Please break the cycle of gangs
Please break the cycle of the lack of positive opportunities
Please break the cycle of nothing to do and nowhere to go
Please break the cycle of abuse and violence
Please break the cycle of killing
Please break the cycle of poverty
Please break the cycle of poor education
Please break the cycle of easy access to guns
Please break the cycle of not enough money to go to college or university
Please break the cycle of parent abandonment
Please break the cycle of drugs in their community (send them away, Lord)
Please break the cycle of unemployment
Please break the cycle of hopelessness

I cut, break, and sever every tie to the curse of the lack of opportunity for today's black youth, off my family line, as well as every black family's line in America.

For my family's part in perpetuating this curse, I ask Lord that You would please forgive us. I choose to forgive my family members (list who and what they did, repent, then you forgive them) and myself (if applies) for not helping black youth reach their potential.
I also choose to forgive this country for its perpetuation of this curse on our black youth.
Lord, please provide every opportunity You desire, to help our black youth succeed. Please restore EVERYTHING the enemy and history have taken away from our youth.
I can't wait to see how You're going to do this, Lord! In Jesus' name. Amen!

66. LEECHES (FOLKS THAT PREY)

Father God, I stand before You, as a representative of my family line. In the name of Jesus, I humbly ask that the curse of leeches (people who prey on me and my family), be removed from our family line.

I cut, sever, and break off all ties to human leeches that prey on our family line. I repent for anything my family members did (white or black), to bring on this curse. I break, cut, and sever all curses that were originally established by my ancestors where we stole from the poor and catered to the rich. I break, cut, and sever all alliances formed by my ancestors, where the spiritual door opened for human leeches to constantly come through and attach themselves to my family members. In the name of Jesus of Nazareth, I close all spiritual doors that my ancestors opened to human leeches. I plead the blood of Christ over me and my family line.

All disingenuous smooth talking to our family members, STOP in the name of Jesus.
I break all spells, trusts, and holds, these leeches seem to have over my family members.
I break the power leeches seem to have in acquiring things from our family that they don't deserve; like trust, time, energy, money, favor, position, and attention.

In the name of Jesus Christ of Nazareth, I pry all leeches off me and my family members:
People who constantly ask for money and never pay us back, leave in the name of Jesus. People who gain access to my loved ones behind my back, leave in the name of Jesus. People who play on our sympathy, but never change, leave in the name of Jesus.
People who borrow items and never return them, leave in Jesus' name.
People who live with us and have no intention of leaving, leave in Jesus' name.

Lord, You command us to love one another. Yet there are leeches out there Lord, who know how to take advantage of us. Lord, give us the words to say to them, the action to match the words, and the strength to stand by our actions. You know what's best for these people. Please break our family members from being their enablers, as we give these mooching souls to You. Please watch over these leeches, and bring them into their own blessings.

Now, let me not be a hypocrite, Lord.
Please forgive me when I leeched on others.
Please forgive me, for every time I asked for money and didn't return it (list and repent). Please forgive me when I played on someone's sympathy and didn't deserve it (list and repent).
Please forgive me when I borrowed things and never returned them (list and repent). Please forgive me when I lived with someone and had no intention of leaving (list and repent).

Please help me show the same mercy, that I was shown.
Bless us to be generous lenders and not bitter borrowers.
However, grant us discernment when to give, and when not to give, always keeping in mind, You are Lord, and judge of us all.

Lord, I choose to give You my anger, every time a leech has taken advantage of me or my family member (list the leech, what they did and forgive).

I choose to forgive every family member for enabling the leeches (list the enabler in the family and forgive).

Lord, I cancel, cut and sever the false sense of security my family members feel, when they needlessly give. I break off their bondage to using their "giving" as a means of empowerment. The excuse "I don't have much (insecurity), but at least I can help so-in-so (power), feed leeches sustenance from our family member's own life supply. In other words Lord, I break, cut and sever all the enablers in my family line, who give to human leeches, because it makes them feel better.

Lord, real leeches inject an anesthesia into their victims when they're feeding on their prey, and suck until they are filled, not giving back any nutrients to their prey. Lord, please don't let these human leeches, dull our minds with their flattering words, keeping us from seeing what they're really doing, and robbing us of our nutrients for daily living. Lord Jesus, please remove all human leeches from our life.

Please restore what the leeches have sucked away from our family line.
Please restore relationships that have been broken between our family members, including myself (if applies). Please wear off the anesthesia human leeches have injected in our family. Help us to wake up, recognize the truth about the leeches in our lives, and pry them loose.
Please give us the right words to say to family members, who don't want to recognize the leeches in their lives.

Please restore our family's trust, rebuild our confidence, and grant us joy, in the places where leeches have stolen our joy, destroyed our trust, and torn down our relationships. Please grant our family, true security in You Lord!
Give us back our family, Lord.
Grant us positive discussions in this matter.
Let those who need to go, GO.
Let those who need to stay, STAY.
Bring back those that need to come BACK.
Restore us to be better than we were, as a family.
Stronger than we were, as a family.
Happier than we were, as a family.
Help us to listen to You, Great God, and not be afraid to obey Your every leading.
In the name of the Father, and the Son, and the Holy Ghost. Amen!

http://en.wikipedia.org/wiki/Leech

67. LETTING EVIL SPIRITS IN

Lord Jesus, You said in Matthew 12:43-45, if a person who doesn't know You, is cleansed of an evil spirit, after not finding any rest, the evil spirit returns, bringing with it seven spirits worse than itself. Leaving the state of the person, worse than before.

So, Father, in the name of Jesus, I ask You to please remove the curse of letting evil spirits in, off my family line.

As a member of this family, I cut, break, and sever all ties to the curse of letting evil spirits in, off my family line, whether accidentally or on purpose.

In the name of Jesus, I send all evil spirits back to the place where Jesus would have them to go. I shut all spiritual doors to portals that have allowed evil spirits to enter, and
I take authority by the Blood of the Lamb that all demons must stay out.

Please help us keep those doors closed, Lord Jesus.

I ask Lord that You would please forgive the person in my family line that introduced the curse of letting evil spirits in to our family. I repent for their sin, and I humbly apologize, Lord, for all their actions. I choose to forgive them, as well.

I also repent for everyone in my family line, who continued to re-introduce this curse to our family. I ask that You would not only forgive their sin in playing around with the occult, but I ask You Lord to please forgive the actions and behaviors that came out of their demonic state.

I ask that You Lord would please seal every spiritual door, window, ceiling, and floor, that opens to any dimensions that let in evil spirits.

I ask that You Lord would protect me, my children, and my children's children, for a thousand generations, from accessing portals where evil spirits may enter them.

Lord Jesus, please grant us wisdom and discernment when we're entertaining wickedness, and the strength to close our eyes, walk away, or even denounce entry, before evil spirits can take hold of us.

Please protect us from evil, Lord Jesus, but remind us to minimize their control, remembering all evil spirits are subject to You, the living Christ. The Risen Lord!

To the Alpha, to the Omega, the Beginning and the End, we are most grateful to You Lord God, that You are on <u>our</u> side. We love You, Lord. In Jesus' name, Amen.

68. LOSS OF CHILDREN

Dear Lord of the Universe, the loss of our children is an unfathomable pain. It's a pain that sears the heart. So Lord, in the name of Jesus Christ of Nazareth, I ask that You would please remove the curse of the loss of children, from my family line.

I break, cut and sever, all ties to the curse of losing children in our family line.
I break, cut and sever, all ties to premature death off our children, in Jesus' name.
I break, cut and sever, all generational alienation by parents, which was passed down from slavery as a coping skill to deal with loss and selling of their children.

Lord, as a member of my family line, I choose to forgive all those that were historically involved in the loss of our children. I forgive all capturers (black and white), jailers, slave shippers, auctioneers, slave masters, governments, Christians (that weren't abolitionists), and all those who participated and profited from the removal and selling of our children.

I give You Lord, all the generations of negative emotions that attached to my family line, every time our children were removed and sold.
I give You Lord, all feelings of loss when our children were taken from us.
I give You Lord, all feelings of powerlessness,
I give You Lord, all feelings of abandonment
I give You Lord, all feelings of guilt for not being able to protect our children.
I give You Lord, all feelings of profound sadness from losing our children
I give You Lord, all feelings of hatred toward our children's capturers.

For the parents in my family, who never saw their children again, Lord,
I give You Lord, all their inconsolable grief and rage.
I give You Lord, all their shut-down mechanisms, including numbness, over-eating or not speaking about the loss ever again.
I give You Lord, all the detachments, indifferences, and abuses they used, as coping mechanisms to deal with their loss of children.
I give You, all these historical behaviors Lord, especially those behaviors that got passed down generationally through our family line, against our children today.

Please Lord, forgive anyone in my family line that participated in the kidnapping and selling of other people's children, whether they were African, European, or Native American. I humbly apologize and repent for their actions. I choose to forgive them, too.

May we love the children You have given us Lord. Please remove the fear from the past, and help us to raise our children in the fear of the Lord. Please bless them into adulthood, and help us to properly let them go when it's time. Lord. I ask that You take charge over our children, guiding their footsteps to good communities where they can flourish, to my children, and to my children's children, for a thousand generations. In Jesus' name. Amen.

69. MAMMY (FOR OVER-WEIGHT WOMEN)

Lord Jesus, please remove the curse of the mammy off my family line. As a member of this family line, I cut, break, and burn, the mammy curse off me and every female in my family line, in the name of Jesus Christ!

I cut, break and sever all mammy imagery, behavior, and stereotypes that have been assigned to us by white society, off my family line, in the name of Jesus Christ!

I discard, in the name of Jesus:
the colorful bandana,
the body fat,
the exuberance of joy to please white people and the master,
the chastising of black youth,
the servant's role as surrogate mother to white children while ignoring our own, OR the over-whelming responsibility of taking care of everyone else's kids in the family,
the need to protect every one, while neglecting ourselves.

Today Lord, we choose to make ourselves the number one priority Lord, because if we don't take care of ourselves, we'll die a premature death.
I cancel all premature death off me.
I cancel nurturing <u>everyone</u> else, except myself.
I cancel all real, fictional, and commercial mammies.
I cancel all imagery that is projected onto me, as a mammy.
I cancel the mammy stigma I've allowed to label me, in order to get along politically,
financially,
economically,
socially,
and spiritually in this society.

I cancel off me, all mammy character traits of being:
big and bosomy,
asexual (yet had lots of kids),
bandana wearing,
apron clad,
domesticated with an unwavering loyalty to whites,
rejected as a beauty,
rejected as an equal in the workforce,
verbally praised for contributions in the workforce, but denied fair compensation,
a colorful but mismatched wardrobe, due to the lack of funds,

I cancel all historical mammy imagery throughout our country as being:
big bare ass as a source of jokes,
farting,

nappy headed,
black man hating,
watermelon eating,
pancake cooking,
diaper washing,
child rearing,
happy slave,
wide grinning,
and a loyal servant.

I renounce the slave curse of not living beyond the age of 50.

I renounce the conjured up imagery of mammy, as a response to abolitionist's protest of slave owner's screwing their female slaves.

I renounce her being deliberately ugly, morbidly obese, and asexual, as a means to preserve the sanctity of the white household, proving to be too unattractive to tempt the white husband.

I ask Lord that You would please forgive all those in American society that contributed to the negative imagery and characteristics of the African-American woman throughout this country's history, even up to today.

I choose to forgive all those in our society that contributed and profited from the mammy caricature. If anyone in my family line contributed to this curse, I choose to forgive them, as well.

Please Lord, root out the mammy caricature from our American culture.
Please restore healthy body imagery in all our black females.
Please restore healthy self-esteem in all our black females.
Please restore healthy community around all our black females, so one woman isn't doing all the work, by herself.
Please restore healthy parameters around all our black females, so no woman dies before her time, from too much stress.

Thank You Lord, for this nation's history of strong African-American women.

I ask You to please restore the respect and praise these women publicly deserve, despite what the mammy caricature tried to rob them of.

Please restore what the mammy caricature has distorted and destroyed throughout American history.

No more mammies, in our family, Lord. To me, to my children, and to my children's children, for a thousand generations. In Jesus' name. Amen.

Dr. David Pilgrim, Professor of Sociology, Ferris State University
www.ferris.edu/jimcrow/mammies

70. NEGATIVE IMAGERY and RACIAL SLURS

Father, in the name of Jesus, I ask that You would break this country from the curse of negative imagery and racial slurs against African-Americans. I ask that You would please remove this curse from my family line.

In the name of Jesus Christ, I break, cut, and sever all ties to the curse of negative imagery of Africans and African-Americans off my family line. I also cancel all the effects those images had on my family line.

I ask Lord, that You would forgive all those, who throughout the centuries of this nation's history, contributed to the negative imagery and racial slurs towards blacks.

As a member of my family line, I choose to forgive all those who historically wrote, drew, printed, reproduced, spray painted, emailed, texted, or tweeted negative black imagery and racial slurs through posters, newsprint, books, newspapers, magazines, letters, flyers, blackboards, billboards, bathroom stalls, any kind of wall or surface, computers, phones and all other forms of media.

I choose to forgive all those in this country, who pushed their negative imagery and racial slurs against African-Americans through: word of mouth, slurs, speeches, jokes, songs, sermons, live presentations on stage, radio and television, recorded pictures, slides, film, albums, videos, cds, dvds, computers, and phones.

I choose to forgive all those in this country who buffooned, belittled, degraded, satirized, published, and performed disgraceful representations of my people in the name of
humor,
social awareness,
education,
or simply as a means of profit.

I also forgive all those in my family line who willingly and unwillingly participated in all forms of negative imagery and racial slurs.

In the name of Jesus, I renounce all imagery and racist slurs of blacks as
monkeys,
baboons,
gorillas,
drug pushers,
pimps,
thugs,
hoes
dead beat dads,
poor,
lazy,

promiscuous,
drug addicts,
criminals,
gangsters,
thieves,
African savages,
people to be feared,
unintelligent
 illiterate
superstitious
over-grown lipped,
over-grown behind,
minstrels,
tap-dancers,
loafing slaves,
watermelon/chicken eaters,
alligator bait (especially naked black babies),
coons (tall, skinny, loose-jointed, slow, poor, self-absorbed, dark skinned oafs)
brutes (angry, strong, animalistic, violent black males)
uncle toms (kind loving servants to whites, intellectually childlike)
mammies (sassy, overweight servants, loyal to white families, neglectful of her own)
picanninies (black babies)
sambos
jigaboos
buckwheat
boy
gal
speartruckers
tarbabies (feel free to add any missing racist terms)
niggers (field and house)

In the name of Jesus, I break, cut and sever, all the roots to the word nigger, which was established in America by the early 1800s. I rebuke and renounce the word nigger, and all its effects off my family line. As a chief symbol of white racism for centuries, I break off all the racist, prejudices, ties, holds, and bondage the word nigger has on my family line, and all black families in America and around the world.

I break, cut and sever every variation of the word nigger used as a reference in America.
In the name of Jesus, I cancel the power in the words--
nigger-- to wear out, spoil, destroy,
niggerish--acting in an adolescent and irresponsible way,
nigger lipping--wetting the end of a cigarette while smoking it,
nigger lover--whites who don't loathe blacks,

nigger luck--exceptional good luck, undeserved,
nigger flicker-small knife or razor with one side taped to preserve one's fingers,
nigger heaven--where blacks were forced to sit, like the balcony in a theatre or court,
nigger knocker--an axe handle, or weapon made out of an axe handle,
nigger rich--someone who's showy, but deep in debt,
nigger shooter--a sling shot,
nigger steak-- a slice of liver or a cheap piece of meat,
nigger stick--a police baton,
nigger tip--leaving a small tip or no tip at all in a restaurant,
nigger milk--a baby drinking ink,
nigger in a wood pile--a concealed motive or unknown fact
nigger work--demeaning, menial tasks.
nigger-brown, nigger-black--the darkest shades of color
Nigger Run Fork, Virginia--small towns,
nigger breaker,
nigger dealer,
nigger driver,
nigger killer,
nigger stealer,
nigger worshipper,
nigger looking,
nigger baby, boy, and girl,
nigger mouth,
nigger preacher,
nigger job,
nigger college,
nigger music--all referring to any association with blacks.

I also renounce the use of the word nigger to put other ethnic groups down:
white niggers—for Irish people; sand niggers--for Arab people;
yellow niggers- for Asian people, etc.

Wow, God. That's a lot of verbal and visual abuse.
I give You all the pain in those centuries of negative imagery and racial slurs.
I give You all the sadness in those centuries of negative imagery and racial slurs.
I give You all the shame in those centuries of negative imagery and racial slurs.
I give You all the needless death, hatred, and persecution that came out of centuries of negative imagery and racial slurs against my people.

I choose to forgive it all, by the power of Jesus Christ of Nazareth.

Lord, please restore to my family line and to all African-American family lines, the respect and dignity that were historically taken away from us.
Only You have the power to do this Lord. In Jesus' name. Amen.

Dr. David Pilgrim, Professor of Sociology, Ferris State University
www.ferris.edu/jimcrow/caricature

71. NIGGER JAILS and HOLDING CELLS

Father, in the name of Jesus, I thank You Lord. I thank You for allowing my family to come through the historic mess called slavery. I thank You for allowing me to stand here today, to praise You that we are still here.

Lord, we know that during the time of slavery, there were holding cells or "nigger jails" that were designed to hold innocent blacks against their will in Africa and America, until they were sold as property.

Once America outlawed importing Africans as slaves in 1807, the price of homegrown slaves, skyrocketed. By the mid 1800's, whether blacks were being sold by slave owners or banks, they were inspected, displayed (in boutiques in Charleston), and auctioned as used goods. In many cases, black families were divided up and sold off, person by person, for maximum profit.

Lord, I ask that You would please remove the curse of nigger jails off my family line. I choose to forgive all those that were involved in humiliating, selling, and pulling my family members apart, for profit or restitution of debt.

Prior to the Civil War, Lord, if any members of my family line were detained, inspected, sold, or died in a nigger jail, then I cut, sever and break all ties of the curse of the nigger jails, off my family line, in the name of Jesus Christ of Nazareth.

Lord I choose to forgive all those involved in placing this curse on my family line, and Lord I ask that You would please break all generational patterns of family members going to jail. Please forgive what they did if they were guilty. Please forgive the authorities and prosecutors, if they were innocent.

As a member of this family, I break, cut and sever the generational patterns of going to jail, off my family line. In the name of Jesus, I break this curse off: (list each family member who's gone to jail, why, and forgive them).

Break, racial profiling. Break, arrests for judicial profits. Break, bad representation. Break, incarceration. Break, repeat offenses. Break addictions. Break old life styles, with bad friends and bad habits. Break, recidivism. Break, fear. Break, enabling. Break anger. Break hatred. Break humiliation. Break hopelessness.

In the name of Jesus, everything that nigger jails robbed, Lord, please, return. Forgiveness, return. Positive community, return. Justice, return. Hope, return. Training, return. Opportunities for making a living, return. Joy, return. Positive contributions to society, return. Prosperity, return.
Lord, please remove going to jail or prison, off our family line, to me, my children, and my children's children, for a thousand generations. In Jesus' name. Amen.

Charleston's Walking Slave Tour – Fall 2012
http://gullahtours.com/gullah/did-you-know-that

72. NOT BEING MARRIED

Father, in the name of Jesus of Nazareth, I come before Your throne, asking that not being married, NOT be looked upon as a curse.

Lord, You are the Author of matrimony. It is Your good pleasure to see people happily married. If people in our family want to get married, and there is a curse, please break the curse of not being married, off our family line, in Jesus' name.

I stand in as a member of this family line, apologizing for anyone in my line who initiated this curse. Please forgive them Lord, and all those that continued to perpetuate this curse.

Lord I choose to forgive all those in my family line that brought dishonor to marriage to our blood line. In the name of Jesus, I cut, break, and sever all curses placed against marriage. (List each family member, their marital misdeed, apologize to God on their behalf, and you forgive them)

Lord, please bring healing back to our family's marriages.
Please bring fidelity back to our marriages.
Please bring dignity back to our marriages.
And for those of us in our family who are not married and wish to be, help us to wait and find the right mate. Help the right mate, to wait and find us.

Lord I break off all links to curses on black marriages from slavery times, where in some places we were not allowed to marry. I choose to forgive all slave capturers, slave brokers, masters, magistrates, legislators, and ministers who participated in this unholy doctrine to serve their own corrupt purposes (including rape and profit). I break every lie from the past, that told slaves they were not worthy of marriage, forcing them to co-habitat without legitimizing their commitment (shacking up).

I forgive all those in my blood-line who were forced to participate in non-committed relationships. I ask Lord, when it comes to marriage, that You would cancel all generational fear, disillusionment, lust, inability to commit, anger, abandonment, pride, detachment, hopelessness, doubt and any other negative behaviors or emotions that attached to my family line during slavery.

I ask Lord that You would please restore healthy and happy marriages to our family's line. Please help us to wait for the right mate, and once we find each other, fully love each other.

Please grant us joy in our marriages. May my family's marriages receive all the blessings they were robbed of, from this nation's past. Only You Lord, have the power to change centuries of damage. Please change the marital structures of our family line, so we may enjoy all that You have designed for us in Holy Matrimony. In Jesus' name. Amen.

73. NOT GETTING ENOUGH CREDIT

Father, in the name of Jesus, please remove the curse of not getting enough credit for the things we do, OFF our family line.

As a member of this family, I break, cut and sever all ties to the curse of not getting enough credit, off my family line.

Lord, I don't know what my family member did, to bring this curse on our family line.
If they stole the credit from someone else, please forgive them. I choose to forgive their actions, as well.

I apologize to You for anyone else in my family who took the credit for other people's accomplishments, and I ask that You Lord would forgive their actions, too.

Lord, I choose to forgive all those in my family line, who not only took what wasn't theirs, but took credit for it.

I choose to forgive the white side of my family, for participating in the stealing, of the black side of my family, purchasing them as stolen goods.

I also choose to forgive the white side of my family, for taking any credit for what the black side of my family accomplished, as their property (like credit for profitable harvests like rice, cotton, and tobacco OR credit for infrastructures of roads and buildings OR economic improvements OR engineering achievements OR medical advances OR musical innovations OR military strategies and so on).

Wow, that's complicated Lord! Please untangle the lines, and help me to pray cohesively.

For every piece of cotton that was turned into beautiful fabric,
for every tobacco leaf that made smoking profitable,
for every grain of rice that was served,
for every brick that was laid and still stands,
for every kind of design, invention, and recipe,
whether it was an idea, plan or fully produced;

if my family members stole the credits for these types of accomplishments
from those who had no power, then I choose to forgive them.

If the accomplishments of my family members were stolen, then I choose to forgive those who stole the credit. Even if this all took place within the black and white blood line of my family.

I choose to forgive the people and events that I know about, where the credit was stolen from our family members, inside or outside the family (list and forgive).

Please forgive me Lord, and all my family members, when we took the credit from people, inside or outside the family (list and ask for forgiveness).

I apologize for not giving YOU, all the credit, all the time, Lord!
Every time You've blessed me, I've sometime taken the credit for myself or credited being lucky.

Please forgive me, Lord.

When You've gotten me out of scrapes, hardships, injuries, financial troubles, family matters, health issues,
You name it, I prayed it and You delivered.

Please forgive me for forgetting to give You the credit, privately and publicly, every time You've saved me!

God, You made EVERYTHING and You don't get all the credit YOU DERSERVE!
Forgive us God, as human beings
for denying our God the credit for the very breath we breathe.
For another day of life.
For life itself.

So it starts today. I'll give You thanks and the credit for all You've done for me.
Thank You Lord for: (thank God for everything He's provided in your life).
Pride, leave.
Anger, leave.
Shame, leave.
Hostility, leave.
Revenge toward those who stole my credit, leave.
The need to receive more credit, leave.
All spiritual blocks that kept me from hearing God's approval, leave.

Joy, return. Self-satisfaction, return and be enough.
May the credit for my accomplishments, return in Your Timing, Lord.
May the credit for all black people's accomplishments in this nation, return, Lord.

You are our God. You are our Creator. You made everything!

When I don't get the credit I think I deserve,
help me not to get upset, Lord.
Because in the end, You Lord, deserve all the credit, anyway! In Jesus' name.
AMEN.

74. NOT LOOKING FOR US, WHEN WE GO MISSING

Father, in the name of Jesus, as a member of this family, and a member of the African-American community, I humbly come before You today, asking that You would please remove from my family line, and all black family lines, the curse of authorities and media, not looking for us, when we go missing.

By the blood of Jesus, I cut, sever, and break all ties to the curse of the police and local news stations, not fully looking for missing African-Americans, like they do for White Americans. I break this curse, off my family line and all African-American families, which started after the abolishment of slavery, when blacks were no longer considered valuable property.

I cut, cancel, and sever all roots of slavery off the black community, where the motivation to look for missing blacks seems to be a waste of time, since we're no longer considered persons of worth.

I apologize for any members of my family line (black or white), that participated in bringing on this curse or re-instating it, throughout our family's history, Lord.

Lord, I choose to forgive all those who participated in placing this curse on our family and community. I choose to forgive all American, African and European slave traders who kidnapped our families from Africa, while their powerless families and communities could do nothing about these abductions, except grieve.

I choose to forgive all those in the American, African and European slave trade, who financially gained from selling our family members, marking their worth, according to the value they deemed appropriate.

I choose to forgive all authorities (police, judges, lawyers, law-makers, vigilantes), that legally contributed to the institution of slavery and made the bounty great, for runaway slaves. I forgive all cruel structures put into place to immediately find and return runaways, yet today, the very opposite reaction happens when we go missing.

I ask You Lord to please reverse today's public response to missing black people. May the high alert to find us, return, within the white community.

I cancel the apathy in our own community, when one of our own is lost or snatched. Please grant our community the awareness to quickly respond to missing persons. Please help us to positively identity a kidnapping and provide accurate information. Please provide us with the power to reach the right people, the right authorities, the right media, and the right hot lines for help, in Jesus' name.

But most of all Lord, we pray to Thee to please bring back our missing loved ones, safe and sound. In Jesus' holy name. Amen!

Tom Joyner Morning Show: for always being responsive to missing black people.DVD: *Patrice O'Neal, Elephant in the Room*, Director Beth McCarthy-Miller (inappropriate for children)

75. NOT RELEASING PEOPLE WHO ARE JEALOUS OF YOU

Father, in the name of Jesus, I ask that You would please remove the curse of not releasing people who are jealous of me.

As a member of this family, I cut, break and sever all ties to the curse of feeling obligated to people who are jealous of me and my family members. I ask Lord that You would please release all physical, financial, and emotional ties to these people, in Jesus' name.

Lord I ask that You would please forgive the person who first introduced this curse onto our family line. I apologize for their actions and repent for what they did. I choose to forgive them as well.

I cancel this curse from my family line, all the way back to when Cain was jealous of his brother Abel (Genesis 4:4), down to when this curse was first introduced to my family line. I repent for everyone in my family that perpetuated this curse.

Lord there are people, right now in my life that I know, who are jealous of me. I cater to them, jeopardizing my mental health, my physical health, my financial wealth, and my primary relationships, by allowing them to bring me down.

Please forgive me for allowing these people more room in my life than they deserve. Please forgive me for trying to be (for them) whatever they want me to be, instead of being the person You've created me to be.

Jealous people in my life, leave. Guilt, leave. Regrets, leave. Fear, leave. Craziness, leave. Distortion, leave. Neediness, leave. Enabling, leave. Excuses, leave.

Lord, please forgive me for catering to the following jealous people (list and forgive yourself).

Lord, please balance out my relationships with the people I care about the most. Lord, please help me to get rid of people who don't care about me.

Grant me the courage, the wisdom, and the resistance to weed the jealous people out of my life.

Freedom, return. Joy, return. Honesty, return. Courage, return. Balanced household, return. Good relationships, return.

Lord, please keep this curse away from our family line, from me, my children, my children's children, for a thousand generations.

In Jesus' name. Amen.

76. OUR FOUNDING FATHERS

Lord God Almighty, thank You for the privilege of coming before Your throne. Thank You Lord Jesus for the direct access You've allowed us to obtain through the shedding of Your Blood on our behalf.

Lord I ask that You would please remove the curse of our Founding Fathers of this country, off my family line.

While I recognize the benefits of their tenacious behavior, to forge a nation of independence, I also recognize their ignorance in not living up to the very creed they formed our government by, "that all men are created equal", seeing that they did not even recognize blacks as fully human.

Lord, I don't wish to cancel the audacity for ambition that built this nation. But I do ask that You would please break off my family line, the curse of ambiguity formed by the Founding Fathers, who built this nation's wealth on the backs of free blacks, indentured servants, and slaves, without sharing the profits of their labor. In other words, they needed us, but they didn't want to acknowledge us. We were subhuman to the people who founded this nation.

I cancel, sever, and burn the roots to the curse of NOT being considered fully human, but only a commodity, off all members of my family line.

I cancel, sever, and burn all roots from the curse of laziness of the wealthy and powerful in this country. I cancel their ability to use their entitlement as an excuse not to work. I cancel the root of influence from the founding of this nation, especially in their treatment toward indentured servants, slaves, slave wages, and even today with unequal pay and benefits in the workforce.

I cancel, sever, and burn all roots to the curse of hierarchies (ranking), that were formed from the beginning of this nation, that carried over from existing imperialist societies from all over the world including Africa, Europe, Asia, North and South America. I break their crowns' impact on establishing an unjust society. I break their effect on our economic unbalance in our society, which constantly taints our democracy.

Please forgive us Lord, for our selfish indulges to keep others down, and please shape our nation to be a place where all Americans can truly be free and equal.

I cancel, sever and burn all roots to undermining and bias laws that were instituted to keep blacks oppressed in this nation.

I break, sever and cancel all moral and religious hypocrisy by the Founding Fathers that claimed their independence from England, yet chose to maintain the institution of slavery.

I break the root curse of BEING DISREGARDED by the British, that served as the catalyst for the Revolutionary War, off our nation.
I break the root curse of ANGER off our nation.
I break the root curse of REBELLION, off our nation.
I break the root curse of PROSPERITY AT ANY COST, off our nation.
I break the root curse of STEALING PEOPLE'S LAND, off our nation.
I break the root curse of INHERENT LAZINESS, off our nation.
I break the root curse of INSECURITY, off our nation.
I break the root curse of NEEDING TO BE ACCEPTED by people who have no intention of accepting us, off our nation.
I break the root curse of the PRETENSE OF SELF-IMPORTANCE, off our nation.
I break the root curse of ENTITLEMENT, off our nation.
I break the root curse of VIOLENCE, off our nation.
I break the root curse of SEGREGATION, off our nation.
I break the root curse of EMASCULATION, off our nation.
I break the root curse of MOBS and MOB MENTALITY, off our nation.
I break the root curse of INFECTIOUS DISEASES, off our nation.
I break the root curse of PRANKS that spur violence and death, off our nation.
I break the root curse of EXPLOITATION OF HUMANS, off our nation.
I break the root curse of FALSIFIED NEWS IN THE MEDIA, off our nation.
I break the root curse of GREED, off our nation.
I break the root curse of TYRANNY, off our nation.
I break the root curse of CORRUPT SYSTEMS, off our nation.
I break the root curse of BROKEN PROMISES, off our nation.
I break the root curse of DOUBLE STANDARDS, off our nation.
I break the root curse of DIVISION BETWEEN OUR STATES, off our nation, asking You Lord, to please unite our States to be a perfect union.

I humbly repent for anyone in my family line that brought these curses to my generational line and I choose to forgive every person that subjected my family line to these root curses.

By the blood of Jesus Christ of Nazareth, I hereby break off all these root curses off my family line, from the time my blood-line arrived on this soil, to this present day. I break all the Founding Fathers' root curses off me, all my living family, my children, my children's children, for a thousand generations.

I give You Lord, all negative emotions tied to these former curses. I give You:
our anger,
our sadness,
all feelings of rejection,
our disgrace,

all feelings of inferiority,
our hatred,
our rebellion (against You and Your will alone),
our injustice,
all times we were ignored,
all times we were taxed unjustly,
all times we were paid unjustly,
all times we were displaced from our homes unjustly
all times we were punished unjustly,
all times we were killed unjustly,
all times we were made to cohabitate unjustly,
slandered
exploited,
separated,
uneducated,
policed,
oppressed,
mobbed,
hung
tortured
humiliated,
robbed,
and dehumanized,
I give You Lord all these emotions, including shame, on behalf of all my ancestors, as a representative of my family line.

And I ask Lord, that You would rectify these emotions with the positive traits that were used by our Founding Fathers, to establish this nation.

I ask Lord that You would please bless our family line with the root blessings of our nation.

Lord, I claim the founding root blessing of the audacity of hope.
Lord, I claim the founding root blessing of prosperity.
Lord, I claim the founding root blessing of defiance, for what is right.
Lord, I claim the founding root blessing of religious freedom.
Lord, I claim the founding root blessing of the underdog, winning when all odds are against us.

And I claim the most important root blessing of all , "In God, We Trust", that being You Lord God.

I claim all these blessings for my family line, for me, for my children, and for my children's children, for a thousand generations, in the name of Jesus Christ of Nazareth! Amen.

DVD: *Liberty! The American Revolution*, Director Ellen Hovde and Director Muffie Meyer

77. PEDOPHILIA (SEXUAL CHILD ABUSE)

Father in the name of Jesus, I humbly come before Your throne, asking You to have mercy on my family line. Please remove the curse of pedophilia off my family line, Lord.

I stand in for all those in my family line, who sexually abused children, or were sexually abused, as children. I cut, break, and sever all curses of pedophilia off my family line.

I ask that You would please forgive any one in my family line, who brought this curse on our family, by engaging in inappropriate touching or sexual acts with children, inside or outside of our family. Lord please forgive anyone in the family who continues this curse.

I choose to forgive every person in my family line who engaged in inappropriate touching or sexual acts with children. (List each family member, what they did, to whom, repent for them, asking God to forgive them, then you forgive them. You don't have to "feel" like forgiving them, but by saying you "choose to forgive", you're turning your will over to God, to let go of the past, and get on with your life.)

I ask that You Lord would please remove the sexual child abusers from our family. May their sin be exposed, may they be put out of our family line, and may they be jailed for their offenses, where they can no longer harm children.

Lord, I stand in our family line and I choose to forgive all adults, outside our family line, that sexually molested our young. Please Lord, forgive them (list each molester, what they did, to whom, repent for them, then you forgive them). Lord, for all those outside my family line, who historically molested the children in our family (slave traders, slave owners, etc), please forgive them.

Lord, You know children are incapable of understanding when they are being molested.
Lord, children don't know how to say no to their perpetrators.
Lord, children don't know when to run away from their perpetrators.
Lord, children don't even know how to report to someone else, that they're being molested.

Lord You know, in most cases, sex abusers are trusted adults around the family, who prey on the affections of vulnerable children. So, in the name of Jesus Christ of Nazareth, I ask that You would please break the pattern of sexual child abusers, taking advantage of the children in our family line.

Lord, by Your healing power, I ask that You would please wash off all the dirtiness on my family line, in the name of Jesus! Lord, please pour down Your cleansing rain from heaven, cleansing us of all unwanted feelings that abusers tainted our family with:

Sexual child abuse, leave in the name of Jesus.
All shame, leave.
All dirty feelings, leave.
All victimization, leave.
All feelings of worthlessness, leave.
All feelings of abandonment, leave.
All sexual depravity, leave.
All sexual dysfunction, leave.
All mental dysfunction, leave.
All paranoia, leave.
All depression, leave.
All inability to cope with life, leave.
All powerlessness, leave.
All depression, leave.
All psychological disturbances, leave.
All inability to be compatible, leave.
All inability to be loveable, leave.
All inability to be intimate, leave.
All inability to trust anyone, leave,
All strong desires for vices, leave.
All bad codependences (drugs, alcohol, food, smoking addictions,), leave.
All blaming of one's self, leave.
All mistrust, leave.

Trust, return.
Love, return.
Appropriate touch, return.
Healthy families, return.
Healthy self-image, return.
Discernment of child molesters, return.
Joy, return.
Healthy sex-life, return.
Justice, return.
God's way of handling these perpetrators, return, Lord Jesus.
Forgiveness return, again, and again, and again.
Peace, return.
Celebration, return.
All good emotions that were stolen by the Enemy, return, in Jesus' name.

Lord. Please break off the curse of pedophilia off my family line, off me, off my children, and off my children's children, for a thousand generations, in Jesus' name. Amen.

Susan A Clancy Ph.D.,*The Trauma Myth*
Aaron Fisher, Michael Gillum, Dawn Daniels, *Silent No More: Victim 1's Fight for Justice Against Jerry Sandusky*

78. PERSONAL FEAR

Father God, in the name of Jesus Christ, I choose to give You all my fear.

Lord please remove the curse of personal fear off me and my family line.

Lord, by the power invested in me, as a member of my family, I break, cut and sever all ties to the curse of fear off our family line.

From the beginning of creation, fear started (Genesis 3) with Adam and Eve's separation from You.

Fear is real. Lord Jesus, please cancel all fear experienced through my family line, from creation, all the way down through time, to my family's permanent separation from their loved ones in Africa.

Lord, please cancel all fear passed down through our family line, as my slave ancestors were abducted from their African communities, thrust into captivity, jailed for deportation, squished into cargo ships, quarantined in camps, (some) held in containers until auction, inspected like animals, and sold into the harsh conditions of slavery.

Through the centuries, Lord please break all curses of fear off my family line, that occurred while they lived through the paralyzing grip of slavery and injustice. After the Civil War, Lord, please break the curse of all fear off my family line. Though our family was legally free, please break the bondage of psychological fear off all my family members that witnessed or experienced terrifying events throughout their lifetime.

I choose to forgive all those that brought suffering on my family throughout the centuries. I ask Lord that You would forgive all those who instilled fear in my family line by keeping them oppressed physically, emotionally, or economically (list and forgive).

Lord please break the fear of every family member today (list and give their fear to God).
Lord please break the fear in me. Lord I choose to give You my fear in—
....being too young or too old
....being too stupid or too smart
....being too tall or too short
....dying alone or being lonely
....not having enough money
....not having enough education
....not being good looking
....not being a good parent
....not being a good child

....not being a good provider
....not being desirable enough
....not being important enough
.....dying
....flying
....bad medicine
....bad people
....bad environment
....not making a difference
....not getting what I want
....not having control over my life!

(These are some examples. Start your own list of what you're afraid of, and keep giving it to God. The more you give Him your list of fears, the closer you'll get to the root of what drives your fears. Then give them all to God.)

I ask You Lord to please restore our family's trust and freedom from fear .
Please replenish Your peace and assurance into every fiber of our being, into
every vessel,
every cell,
every bone,
every artery,
every vein,
every joint,
every muscle,
every tissue,
every memory,
every tear,
every smile, Lord.

Please replenish in me, Lord
Your joy,
Your confidence,
Your courage and
Your strength.

Help me to see every failure,
as a new opportunity.
Every disaster I survived,
as Your miracle.
Every mistake I've made,
as an opportunity for Your grace to forgive me.

I give You Lord, all these fears, in the name of the Father, and the Son, and Holy Spirit. In Jesus' name. Amen and Amen!

79. PIMPING and BEING PIMPED

Father, in the name of Jesus, I ask that You would please remove the curse of pimping and being pimped off my family line.

I cut, sever, and break all ties to the curse of pimping and being pimped off my family line, in the name of Jesus Christ of Nazareth.

Lord, I humbly apologize for the actions of any family member that initiated these curses, and all those that followed in my family that continued to participate in these curses. Please forgive all their actions Lord, and I repent to You Lord, for every deed and sin that was conducted against Your will.

I'm sorry Lord for the things, they did against You and against their fellow man and woman. I'm sorry for all my family members pimping others for their own gain. I'm sorry for the humiliation and exploitation that took place before Your very eyes, Lord.

I choose to forgive all those outside our family line, that pimped our family. I choose to forgive all those in the slave industry, shippers, slave traders and slave masters (African, European, and all others) for pimping my family members, in Jesus' name.

Lord I cancel any and all binding contracts that kept my family members bound to pimping or being pimped, in Jesus' name.

I choose to list and forgive all family members that were involved in either actions. Please Lord, bring all family pimps to mind, so I may repent and forgive them all.

Pimping, leave. Being pimped, leave. Anger, leave. Shame, leave. Hopelessness, leave. Vanity, leave. False power, leave. Conniving, leave. Lack of control, leave. Imprisonment, leave. Isolation, leave. Inability to think, leave. Doubt, leave. Being trapped, leave. Chains, leave. Cruel punishment, leave. Harmful lust, leave. Ranking, leave. Identity in sexual prowess, leave. Power from sexual activity, leave. Masks, leave. Greed, leave. Exploitation, leave. Being manipulated, leave. Powerlessness, leave. Inability to say NO, leave. Abandonment, leave.

I choose to forgive my friends for pimping me.
I choose to forgive my family members for pimping me.
I choose to forgive my job for pimping me.
I choose to forgive my spouse or significant other for pimping me.

In the name of Jesus, all pimping, legal and illegal, break off me, my children, and my children's children for a thousand generations.
Real protection come.
Real power come, through Jesus Christ our Lord and Savior. In Jesus' name. Amen.

80. PROCRASTINATION

Lord, there seems to be a problem in my family line with people avoiding doing what they're supposed to do. It may be a generational curse of procrastination. Father, if this is true, in the name of Jesus, I ask that You would please remove the curse of procrastination off my family line.

I cut, break, and sever all ties to the curse of procrastination off my family line. Lord, I don't know who in my family introduced this curse, but I ask that You Lord would please forgive them. I choose to forgive them as well.

It may be that procrastination in my family was introduced, as a response to the brutal work they endured is slaves. Procrastination may have been used as a tactic to combat slavery, and in my family's way, empowered them from exploitive workloads.

It's an understandable tactic. However I now give that tactical maneuver back to You Lord and ask that You would please replace it with a heart to work, whole heartedly.

Lord, I choose to forgive the oppressors that forced the hand of my family to procrastinate. I ask Lord that You would please lift the curse of procrastination off me, my children, and my children's children for a thousand generations.

I choose to forgive (list family members) for procrastinating over (list what was left undone, ask God's forgiveness, then you forgive them). Lord, I choose to forgive myself for procrastinating over (list, ask God's forgiveness, then forgive yourself).

Procrastination, leave in Jesus' name. Fear of failure, leave. Doubt, leave. Sadness, leave. Depression, leave. Powerlessness, leave. Laziness, leave. Anger, leave. Lack of motivation, leave. Hopelessness, leave. Obsession with perfection, leave. Distractions, leave. The haunting of past failures, leave. Regret, leave.

Lord, I give You my procrastination. Is there anyone I need to forgive, before I start my work again? I choose to forgive the following people (list anyone you're holding a grudge against and forgive them, including if you're mad at God).

Lord I choose to forgive myself when I've been judged by others for past failures regarding my work. I choose to forgive those who judged me. I choose to forgive You Lord for not assisting me when I wanted help, the way I wanted it. Please forgive my insolence, Lord. I ask for Your help Lord, to please help me complete my work, Your way, not mine.

Forgiveness return, in Jesus' name. Hope, return. Flow of ideas, return. Joy, return. Purpose, return. Opportunity, return. Goals, return. Faith, return. Motivation, return. Accomplishments, return. Success, return! In Jesus' holy name. Amen.

81. PROSTITUTION

Father, in the name of Jesus, I ask that You would please lift off the curse of prostitution off my family line.

I cut, sever, and break all ties to the curse of prostitution off my family line.

I humbly apologize to You Lord, on behalf of the family member(s) that introduced this curse to our family line. I ask that You would please forgive them for offending You and forgive any other family members that participated in the sin of prostitution.

I also choose to forgive the initiator(s) of this curse for their actions, and for all family members that participated in the curse of prostitution, as well. (List those in the family who were prostitutes, or received money or favors for sex, ask God to forgive them, then you forgive them).

Lord, please forgive me (if applies) for anytime I received money or favors for sex (list, ask God for forgiveness, then forgive yourself).

Prostitution, leave. Shame, leave. Denial, leave. Fear, leave. Anger, leave. Sadness, leave. Depression, leave. Poor self-esteem, leave. All addictions, leave. Lack of opportunity, leave. Lack of money, leave. Bad environment, leave. Co-dependence, leave. Abuse, leave. Exploitation, leave.

Forgiveness, return.
Hope, return.
Self-esteem, return.
New life, come.
New opportunities, return.
New work, return.
Joy, return.
Love, return.
Self-worth, return.
Good self-efficiency, return.
Happiness, return.
Self-fulfillment, return.
Independence, return.

I renounce all the repercussions of prostitution off our family line and I ask Lord that You would please restore everything this curse damaged, throughout our family line.

Lord, please repair and preserve my family line from predators and situations that bring this curse about. I ask this Lord for me, my children, and my children's children, for a thousand generations. In Jesus' name, Amen.

82. RACIAL HIERARCHY

Father, in the name of Jesus', I ask that would You please remove the curse of racial hierarchy in this country.

In the name of Jesus, I cut, sever and break all ties to the social ranking of power in this country, where white people are on the top and black people are on the bottom.

In the name of Jesus, I cut, sever and break all ties to the caste systems of American Slavery and the Jim Crow laws. In the name of Jesus, I fully receive for my family line the credence in the constitution of the United States of America, "that all men are created equal".

In the name of Jesus, I break, cut, and dismantle every societal institution that offered legitimacy to the American racial hierarchy.

In the name of Jesus, I dismantle the lies and forgive every minister in this country that preached that God cursed blacks, to be servants and slaves.

In the name of Jesus, I dismantle the lies and forgive all scientific theory and experiments (on black skulls, brains, faces, genitals), seeking to prove whites were genetically superior to blacks.

In the name of Jesus, I dismantle the lies and forgive all academia (primary, middle and high school teachers, university professors, scholars, and students) who endlessly taught that blacks were less evolved than whites.

In the name of Jesus, I dismantle the lies and forgive all entertainment media from live performances outdoors, indoors, saloon halls, circus tents, theatres, vaudeville acts, film, albums, radio, television, video, cd, dvd, the internet, and all future forms of media, who portrayed blacks as sassy servants, happy-go-lucky idiots, minstrels, or dangerous thugs.

I rebuke, renounce, and dismantle all aspects of the criminal justice system, which sanctions a double standard of justice, including in the past, its tacit approval of mob violence against blacks (lynching, dragging, burnings, and bombings).

I forgive all the anti-black imagery throughout the centuries that supported the hierarchy of white supremacy in this country.

I forgive the negative images of blacks with bulging eyes, bulging lips, huge grins, bandana wearing, shoe shinning, poorly dressed or naked, big breasted, clowning, happily serving whites, can't read, can't write, can't speak English, head scratching, watermelon eating, and any other negative images of blacks that I can think of.

I forgive these and more anti-black images being on everyday products like:

toys, (Darkey Ten Pins bowling set, Greedy Nigger Boy coin toss)
dolls (pickanninies),
books (Ten Little Niggers by Agatha Christie, Little Black Sambo),
puzzles (Chopped up Niggers),
food products (Aunt Jemima, Uncle Ben's, Cream of Wheat),
tobacco (NiggerHair Smoking Tobacco),
house hold items (Mammy cookie jars, salt and pepper shakers, writing pads),
songs, and games (eeny-meeny-miny-moe, catch a nigger by his toes),
expressions ("last one in, is a nigger!")
and so on……

Don't pray this, unless you mean it.

I ask Lord that You would please forgive me for using the word nigger against my own people.
I'm sorry for every time I used the word in any kind of variations (nigga, niggah, niggaz) referring to all blacks, friend or foe.

Please forgive me for using the excuse that the word nigga, is not related to the word nigger, and is meant as a term of endearment. Both words continue to be a term of ridicule.

When You made us, Heavenly Father, Your intent was NOT for blacks to be defined as niggers, no matter their behavior, income, ambition, clothing, ability, or skin tone.

I don't believe popular thought among my people that the sting of the word nigga isn't as hurtful, when used in the right context.

I rebuke the lie, that the more we use the word nigga, the less it's offensive.

I break the lie that nigga is not the same word, because whites say "nigger" and we say "nigga".

I cancel the lie that it's okay to use nigga, because it's just a word.
I cancel the lie that it's okay to use nigga, because blacks shouldn't be prisoners to words from the past.

Lord, since the beginning of slavery, we have internalized the negative images that white society planted and propagated about black skin and black people, throughout the centuries.

Using the word nigga may reflect my own self-loathing (hating myself for being black).
Using the word nigga may reflect my loathing of my race (hating other blacks).
Using the word nigga may be amusing, but it can also be psychologically damaging.

I understand that the word nigger is the ultimate expression of white racism and superiority, no matter how it's pronounced.

I repent for using the word in my everyday language.
I repent for my constant use of it.
I repent for allowing it to internalize negativity about myself and others.

I ask that all the hatred I've attached to the word,
all the love I attached to the word,
be banned from me, cut loose and abandoned by me.

May the words I have for my family, black friends, black foes, or myself, be only words that edify the soul, Lord.

I ask Lord that You would change my negative language to positive language.

I ask You to please change my negative concept about myself to a positive concept of myself.

I renounce all self-loathing and loathing of other blacks.

I ask that You, Lord Jesus would please replace the word nigga, with the word brother.
Please replace words of cursing, with words of blessings.
May I no longer gain humor from that word.
May I accept the fact that the word nigga, is and always will be, an ugly word, in American history.

****

I renounce all the hatred and repulsion that these words and images carried out throughout the world toward my people.

I choose to forgive all the people who called me and my family members, niggers.

I choose to forgive all the corporations that pushed racist black imagery on their products.

Lord, I ask that You would repair all the damage that was committed psychologically, emotionally, spiritually, and physically to my family line.

Please restore Lord, all that was robbed from us by anti-black imagery, replacing it with dignity and honor to all African-Americans, to us, to our children, and to our children's children, for a thousand generations. In Jesus' holy name. Amen.

Dr. David Pilgrim and Dr. Phillip Middleton, *"Nigger and Caricatures"* Article
http://www.ferris.edu/htmls/news/jimcrow/caricature
YouTube: *"Ten Most Racist Toys Ever Made"*

83. SELF-DESTRUCTION

Father God, in the name of Jesus, I humbly come before Your throne asking that You would please remove the curse of self-destruction off my family line.

Standing in as a representative of my family line, I cut, break and sever all ties to the curse of self-destruction, off my family line.

I choose to forgive all those who inflicted this curse on my family. I understand, from the time of the abduction of my family members from Africa, hopelessness was instilled and perpetuated in my family line. Some of my family members made it in life, some of them didn't.

Lord, I go all the way back to the generation that was kidnapped from Africa. I choose to forgive our kidnappers, African and European slave traders. I forgive the slave investors, the ship crews, the prison camps, slave brokers, the masters that owned my people, the laws that enforced slavery, the Christians that did nothing, the owners who separated and sold our family off, all under harsh conditions.

I forgive an unforgiving system of laws that held my family back and stacked the laws against their progress. I forgive centuries of racism in this country, and I forgive those who profited from it. I forgive all those in my family line, who gave up trying to overcome this life in America. I forgive all those who didn't have the skills to survive. All those who didn't make it, because they couldn't make it. I forgive all those, who, when they finally were given a chance, were so damaged, they self-destructed.

I forgive all those, who were responsible for the demise (downfall or death) of my family members (list and forgive).

I break all self destructive oaths, lies, agreements, and contracts off my family line.
I break all survivor's guilt off my family line, in Jesus' name.
I break off the belief that by destroying things OR ourselves, it gives us power.

Self-destruction, leave. Shame, leave. Anger, leave. Fear, leave. Hopelessness, leave. Self-hatred, leave. Survivor's guilt, leave. Abandonment, leave. Betrayal, leave. Depression, leave. Envy, leave. Guilt, leave all in the name of Jesus.

Lord, Your power is <u>love</u> driven.
The power of the enemy of our soul, is <u>hate</u> driven (John 10:10).
By the blood of Jesus Christ of Nazareth, I cut all of Satan's hold off my family line, to me, to my children, and to my children's children, for a thousand generations.
God's power, return!
Lord, please cleanse our family line with Love.
Love return. Love return. Love return. In Jesus' name. AMEN!

84. SELF-DESTRUCTIVE GUILT

This is a curious request Lord. I'm asking You to please remove the curse off our family, for being made to feel guilty by others, for being more successful.

Hear what I'm saying. I'm not asking You to remove Godly humility from our family. No. I'm asking You to please remove all self-destructive guilt, that we allow people to make us feel, for having more than they do. I'm asking You Lord to cancel the kind of guilt that leads to self-destructive behavior (for example, you buy a new car and your jealous friends put you down, so out of guilt, you get drunk and smash your car).

I cut, break, and sever all ties to the curse of self-destructive guilt over being better off than others. All false humility must leave, in Jesus' name.

I ask that You would forgive the family member who originally introduced this curse onto our family. I repent for this act of false humility and self-destructive guilt.

If white family members prospered from doing wrong, like slave trading, owning slaves, prospering from the productivity of slaves, raping slaves, fathering slaves and not claiming them, then I repent for their actions and apologize. I choose to forgive them, and all other family members that have contributed to this curse.

Sin brought onto our family's wealth, leave in Jesus' name.
Entitlement, leave.
Sin against humanity, leave.
Self-destructive patterns, leave.
Need to please people, leave.
Survivor's guilt, leave
Need to control, leave.
Guilt, leave.
Anger, leave.
Shame, leave.
False humility, leave.
Over-compensation, leave.
Destructive patterns, leave.
Sadness leave. All, in Jesus' name.

Lord I repent for any self-destructive behavior I'm aware of, that I or my family members committed (list any time you or a family member did something negative when receiving something prosperous, forgive them and yourself).

I cancel self-destructive guilt from when it first began in my family line, all the way to me, to my children, and to my children's children, for a thousand generations. In Jesus' name. Amen.

85. SELF-DESTRUCTION ONCE I'VE MADE IT

Dear Lord Jesus, what drives me to hurt myself (food, alcohol, drugs, relationships, promiscuous behavior), once I've made it in this world? Why do I do things that hurt myself, my relationships, jeopardizing my career or my quality of life?

Lord, in the name of Jesus, I don't understand my actions, but I choose to cut, break, and sever all ties to self-destructive behavior.

I'm asking You to please put in my path, someone trustworthy that I can talk to, so I can be healed from this behavior.

I understand, that this pattern of self-destruction is rooted in something greater than myself. Lord I ask that You would reveal it to me, and help me to STOP these actions that are leading me down a path to destruction and death.

Lord, I break off all curses of self-destructive living off me and my family's line.
I choose to forgive anyone in my family line that engaged in destructive behavior.
I choose to forgive those who were never able to recover from the prejudices and injustices in this country, and turned to self-destructive behavior in order to cope with their grief.
I choose to forgive all those in my family who felt guilty for thriving in this country, despite the blatant and covert racism of this land.
While they made the best of their circumstances, reaching and exceeding their goals in life, they chose self-destructive behavior, to appease their guilt for being successful.
I forgive them Lord, and I ask You to please forgive them, and me, when I've chosen to engage in self-destructive behavior.

Lord I give You all my guilt about being successful. I give You all my guilt about not helping people I believe I'm supposed to help. I give You my guilt about helping people, when they turned out worse. I give You all my anxiety over being successful, whether it's worrying about staying on top, or worrying about it all being taken away.

Lord, I also choose to forgive myself, on how I made it. Whether I feel I don't deserve my success, or it came too fast, I choose to let my guilt go.

Whether I feel I was underhanded or I hurt people on my way to the top, I choose to forgive myself, and ask Lord that You would forgive me.

Lord, I'm not looking to lose all that You've given me, including my life.
Please bring healing Lord to my situation.
Help me to love those around me, and be a blessing to them, as well.
You've already blessed me, Jesus.
Please help me to enjoy it! In Christ's name. Amen.

86. SELF-PITY

Dear Lord, please forgive me and my family, when we fall into self-pity. If this is a curse, I humbly ask that You would please remove it from our family line.

I, as a member of this family, cut, break, and sever all ties to the curse of self-pity off my family line.

Lord, I choose to forgive the person in my family, who introduced this curse to our family. I ask Lord, that You would please forgive them.

If self-pity came on my family line, as a result of being enslaved for centuries, Lord, I hold no ill will against my family members. Self-pity would have been a natural response to their situation.

Lord, I choose not to hold grudges against the people in the past, who invoked my family members to pity themselves. Instead, I choose to forgive our oppressors. And I ask You Lord, to please forgive them.

I ask You Lord Jesus, God of the supernatural, to please break our family's pattern of self-pity. We might not have been able to stop the pattern from developing in our family, but You sure have the power to break it!

Self-pity, break. Self doubt, break. Sadness, break. Depression, break. Self-loathing, break. Voices in my head that tell me I can't do it, break. Voices in my head that tell me I'm worthless, break. Voices in my head that tell me to give up, break, in Jesus' name. Voices in my head that tell me I don't deserve it, break. Break! Break! Break!

Bad memories from the past, leave. Hurting comments from the past, leave. Damaging parents, guardians, or teachers' comments, leave. The haunting of bad decisions, leave. All betrayals from loved ones leave, in Jesus' name.

Father, in the name of Jesus, I choose to forgive the following people in our family, that perpetuated self-pity (list and forgive, including yourself). Lord, I choose to forgive all circumstances in which we pitied ourselves.

Self-worth, return. Joy, return. Determination, return. Strength, return. Wisdom, return. Discernment, return. Love, return. Gratitude, return. Contentment, return.

Lord Jesus, please remove the cloak of self-pity off my family line.

Please place on me, my children, and my children's children, a robe of confidence, clothed by Your Holy Spirit! In Jesus' name. Amen.

87. SERVANTS SEEN and NOT HEARD

Father, in the name of Jesus, I ask that the curse of servants being seen and not heard, be lifted off my family line.

This was a practice of Europeans and Africans long before they set foot on these shores. Therefore, this curse came over on the boats.

I cut, break, and sever all ties to the curse of servants being seen and not heard, off me and my family line, on both black and white sides of my family tree.

I choose to forgive the person(s) who introduced this curse on to our family line.

I choose to forgive every person of privilege who implemented this curse; be they a royal, landowner, serf owner, slave owner, master of the house, mistress of the house, taskmaster, captain of industry, captain or merchant of the sea, overseer, foreman, boss or designer of the constitution.

Servants (free or slave) in America were counted as nothing, and their only job was to cater to their masters' and employers' households. The owners lived by the motto, servants were meant to serve and be invisible. Those of privilege in the 1700s even designed and built their homes to accommodate this curse, with passageways so they didn't have to see their servants coming or going.

This curse has certainly trickled down through the centuries of American culture, both in the workplace and social settings. People don't talk to "the help".

Well Lord, I'm asking You to change all that. I'm asking You to please abolish the curse of servants not seen or heard, off our nation. I ask You Lord to allow servants to have fair and proper access to their employers.

Lord, from this day forward, no matter what job I have, or my children have, I ask that we would not be invisible to our employers, anymore. I pray, in the name of Jesus, that You would allow us the ability of direct access to the people at the top. I pray we'd never be seen as dispensable, ever again.

Lord please break off the curse of us being only a means to an end, with our only value to our employers being how well we serve them.

Make us visible to our employers.
Make our presence aware to our bosses.
Let our true value be seen by the people for which we work.
Let our employers not see us as a commodity, but as a treasure.
In Jesus' holy name. Amen.

Fairmount Park House Tours *Woodford Mansion*, Philadelphia, Pennsylvania 2011

88. SEXUAL SIN

(Not everyone has had a bad sexual experience. But if there's something in your past that you've experienced, or witnessed, now's the time to get rid of it. While praying:
1. If an event comes to mind that's really painful, you need to stop, take your time,
and forgive every aspect of that memory
2. If a person who assaulted you, is not on the list or in any category in this prayer, but they come to mind, please stop reading the list, and deal with your experience, by forgiving the person and the situation.

Remember, this prayer is not an exact method. It's a way to allow to you to empty out your bad sexual memories, by the power of Jesus Christ.

SO, let's call it out, give it to God, and get rid of it, in Jesus' name. Amen.)

Father, I come to You in the name of Jesus, asking that You would please remove the curse of sexual sin off my family line.

I ask that You would please forgive all those in my family line that initiated or participated in sexual deviancy, whether it was consensual (permitted) or not.

I ask that You would please forgive all sexual predators that flirted, fondled, molested or raped members in my family line (list and forgive).

I ask that You would please forgive any sexual sin I've participated in (list and forgive).

For those sexual incidences in my family, that I may not know about, or have forgotten, I ask that You would please forgive all the following sex acts that were performed by my family members (the guilty) or with my family members (the victim), with or without their consent:

Please Lord Jesus forgive the following sex acts, if they apply to my family:

watching pornography (magazines, television, movies, videos, dvds, internet, sex shows, or any other form of media or technology), buying sex, hurtful sex, degrading sex, aphrodisiacs without consent, having sex with STDs or AIDS without informing partners, public performances of stripping or sex acts, public nakedness, sexual fantasies of others while participating with partners, adultery, incest, all non consensual (without permission) sex, including touching, petting, oral, anal, and sexual harassment (kids giving permission, does NOT make it okay to have sex with them), molesting, raping, fornicating with neighbors, married friends, mothers, fathers, step-mothers, step-fathers, sisters, brothers, cousins, nieces, nephews, uncles, aunts, grandfathers, grandmothers, boyfriends of family members, girlfriends of family members, sexual abuse of children from birth to

1 month, 2 months, 3 months, 4 months, 5 months, 6 months, 7 months, 8 months, 9 months, 10 months, 11 months, age 1, age 2, age 3, age 4, age 5, age 6, age 7, age 8, age 9, age 10, age 11, age 12, age 13, age 14, age 15, age 16 age 17 age 18, strangers, toddlers, preschoolers, elementary students, middle school students, high school students, non consensual sex with: college students, young adults, twenty year olds, thirty year olds, forty year olds, fifty year olds, sixty year olds, seventy year olds, eighty year olds, ninety year olds, military personnel, church elders, pastors, deacons, choir directors, choir members, church goers, doctors, nurses, teachers, professors, business associates and the list goes on (name anyone not mentioned, where non consensual sex took place).

I choose to forgive those people who made me feel like a sex object (list).
Please forgive me Lord, for making people feel like sex objects (list).
Please forgive my family members for making people feel like sex objects (list).

I choose to forgive those in my family line who castrated themselves or others for pleasure, revenge, unholy religious oaths, secret sects, or spite.

I choose to forgive those who castrated people in my family line, no matter the reason. Especially those ancestors who tried to escape from slavery, but were caught and castrated.

I cut, break, and sever all ties of the curse of castration and impotency off my family line and I ask Lord in the name of Jesus, that You would restore full potency to all males in my family line that are living today, to our children, and to our children's children, for a thousand generations.

If I was molested, raped, or violated, in the name of Jesus, I choose to forgive my perpetrator(s), (list and forgive).

I choose to forgive what happened in the places where I was molested or raped, like the den, bedroom, backyard, garage, basement, hall closet, classroom closest, etc.
I choose to let You Lord Jesus, clean those places, by Your Blood.
(If you see that place as a "dirty place", you are NOT going to live the rest of your life with that image! Let Jesus cleanse all areas that you feel are dirty, by the power of His blood).

In the name of Jesus, I break, cut, and sever all ties to the promises I made to my perpetrator or others, that I would never tell my mother, father, or any other person in authority, about what they did to me. I cut all packs and agreements to protect his or her identity, and I forgive myself for making those promises, even if I was only a child.

I forgive my perpetrator(s) for asking me to join in with such a promise, thereby making me feel like an accomplice in their sex act. Whether I agreed, disagreed, or

was too afraid, not to agree with my perpetrator(s), I cleanse myself from any promises I made to them.
I am released from protecting them, by the Blood of Jesus Christ.
Coerced promises, leave.
Guilt, leave.
Confusion, leave.
Fear of betrayal, leave, in Jesus' name.

In the name of Jesus, I cleanse myself of all negative feelings attached to the assault.
Dirtiness, leave.
Guilt, leave.
Depression, leave.
Confusion, leave.
Suicidal tendencies, leave.
Hate, leave.
Jealousy of others' happiness, leave.
Irritability, leave.
False sense of self, leave.
Lying, leave.
Lust, leave.
Anger, leave.
Sadness, leave.
Blame, leave.
Lack of worth, leave.
Sexual innuendos (behavior, comments, pranks), leave.
Self-destructive tendencies, leave in the name of Jesus.

Lord, I choose to forgive myself, if I have been blaming myself for the assault. Even if I technically <u>know it wasn't my fault</u>, I choose to let You release me from the blame of the assault. I choose to give You Lord, all the pain in my assault, Lord Jesus.

Lord, what do You want me to believe about that situation? (Listen. Listen to what He has to say to you.)

Lord, I choose to forgive my mother, my father, and whoever else that should have been in charge of me, at the time of my assault. I choose to forgive them for abandoning me in my time of need. Anger, leave. Betrayal, leave. Fear, leave.

Lord, I choose to forgive You God, for allowing this to happen to me, when I was too young, too afraid, too helpless to help myself. Where were You Lord? (Wait. Wait and see what the Lord shows you.)

I ask You Lord Jesus to restore unto me, ALL that the Enemy stole from me, during those sexual acts.

Please Lord, restore:
my virtue,
my faith,
my love of life,
my love for holy sex,
my joy,
my trust,
my peace of mind,
my security within,
my healthy love of self,
my respect for the body of others,
my appreciation for my own body.

Please restore all my self-worth and show me how to love the way You love me. Restore unto me, Your Joy and Appreciation that I am wondrously made by You, and enable me to feel all Your Love for me, Lord.

Here's the hard part.
I choose to bless, not curse my perpetrator(s), in the name of Jesus.
I choose to release each and every one of them from my very being.
I choose to release everyone I've held captive in my heart, for the wrongs they did to me. I choose to forgive every act they did to me, and I give them to You, Lord, to do as You will.

(If you are a perpetrator, you must ask forgiveness before God Almighty for all the violations you committed.)

During Slavery
Lord, I stand in the gap of my family ancestors (white or black), asking You to please forgive those who participated centuries ago in sexual sin, bringing Your wrath on our family line. I apologize for their actions.

Please forgive all those who angered You, and re-established any sexual curses and addictions by committing: adultery, incest, witchcraft for sex, murder for sex, pimping (those who sold men, women, and children for sex), use of others as sexual objects, blackmail for sex, bestiality, slavery, sexual torture, all sexual perversions, sexual humiliation, sexual manipulation, the robbing of others' virginity, taking of innocence, and being responsible for the wreckage of lives that resulted from their sin.
If this happened, I choose to forgive the use of the females in my family line as sexual objects, the minute they were abducted from Africa. I forgive all their assailants, in Jesus' name.

I choose to forgive all masters (inside or outside the family line) for secretly or overtly bedding their slaves, whether they were married or not.

I choose to forgive all white males, who raped, seduced, blackmailed, beat and continually sexually assaulted the women in my family line, leaving them mentally, physically, and emotionally torn.

I choose to forgive all white males for only seeing our women as sexual objects and laborers.

I ask You Lord to remove all the shame and confusion off my female slave ancestors, over conflicting sexual emotions with their masters. Although they did not initially want their master's sexual advances, they may have fallen in love with their masters. And yet my ancestors may have experienced confusion, once their master's rejected them, by turning their affections back to their wives, or toward other female slaves. Shame, leave. Confusion, leave. Competition, leave. Rage, leave. Rejection, leave. Jealousy, leave. Powerlessness, leave. Abandonment leave, in the name of Jesus.

I choose to forgive all masters' wives who knew about their husbands' sexual conduct with their slaves and did nothing. I ask Lord that You would remove the generational curse of animosity between white women and black women, where there is rivalry over American men.

Please forgive all sexual acts between slave owners (inside or outside of my family line) and slaves, where black men in my family line had to stand aside, and watch their women being sexually assaulted by white men.

I ask Lord that You break the sexual patterns of the male slaves in my family line being used as studs, going from one slave to another, in order to produce more slaves for their masters. I break cut, and sever the generational sexual curse of breeding, off my family line. I ask Lord that You would restore the men in my family line to be endearing and monogamous (faithful) to their wives.

I choose to forgive all those in my family line who were mutilated, castrated, dismembered, burned, tarred, whipped, stripped, beat, pulled apart by ropes, jailed, sold, witnessed their children being sold, or their spouse being sold, or any other loved one being sold, due to sexual accusations, or refusals to having sex.

<u>After the Civil War</u>
If this happened Lord, I choose to forgive anyone for falsely accusing any of my family members of sexual misconduct, by killing them, torturing them, or lynching them, like in the Emmet Till case where he was brutally tortured and killed for whistling at a white woman.

Lord, I forgive all those who falsely or unjustly sentenced my family members to serve for sexual crimes. I forgive all those, who made our family suffer due to their sentencing.

I forgive all those in my family line who were mutilated, castrated, dismembered, burned, tarred, hung, beaten, pulled apart by ropes, or jailed, due to false sexual accusations, or for refusing to have sex with someone.

Lord I forgive all those who persecuted my family in the 19th, 20th, and 21st centuries, for our refusal to bed them, their friends, family, or business associates.

I forgive all those who, under the law, were able to punish my family members, even though my family members were innocent.

Lord, please wash the effects of this sexual curse and addiction off my line, by the blood of the Lamb, breaking all soul ties throughout our family's improper sexual history.

Lord would You please restore our family line with all that was robbed from us, Lord.

By the Blood of the Lamb, I break, cut, and sever all ties to the guilt and pain of these assaults.

I renounce all pain that has had my family bound, and command it to leave, in Jesus' name.

We are cleansed by the Blood of the Lamb, and are new creatures in Christ.

I am now FREE!

I hold no account to any perpetrator, by the blood of the Lamb.

I claim, I am a new child in Christ, cleansed by the Holy Spirit. In the name of Jesus Christ of Nazareth. Amen and Amen.

(If you're still feeling dirty, there's someone/something you've missed. Go back and ask God to show you what you missed. Forgive all that He brings to mind. This might take you a few times, before it's all gone.

Sometimes, it's hard to forgive people who have hurt you badly.
Remember, forgiving them, doesn't mean you're condoning the act.
You are actually freeing yourself from your own spiritual prison of pain.

This is obedience to God, not an exercise in the warm-fuzzies.
As you "choose" to forgive your perpetrators, submitting your will to God, releases the healing in your spirit to let go of the past. The Lord will handle the rest.
Trust God. Be free.)

Dr. Edward M. Smith, *Genuine Recovery*
Chris Crowe, *Getting Away with Murder*

89. SKIN COLOR WAR

Lord, in the name of Jesus, I ask that You would please remove the curse of the skin color war of African-Americans off my family line.

I cut, sever, and break all ties to the curse of the skin color war, off my family line. As a member of this family, I renounce all attachments to the curse of skin tone preference or prejudice.

Lord, I choose to forgive the Europeans, especially the British, who indoctrinated the ranking of skin color among their colonies.

I choose to forgive all the slave masters that raped and fathered illegitimate children with their slaves, only to deny them the benefits of their masters' birthright.

I choose to forgive all slave rankings, which placed higher value on blacks that were lighter in skin tone, granting them favoritism in labor, social ranking, and in other levels of American society.

Lord I choose to forgive the family member that introduced this curse to our family line, whether the skin color war evolved from the rape and birth of a slave family member, the selling of a family member, or hostility over preferential treatment of light skin slaves over dark skin slaves. I repent for my ancestors' (black and white) actions and reactions, Lord. I ask that You would please forgive them.

Lord, if I have offended You by ridiculing African-Americans about their skin tone, I'm sorry. If I have offended Thee, by making preferential treatment for people based on their skin tone, please forgive me Father God. I apologize to You for my behavior, and ask You to please forgive my racist acts.

I choose to forgive the following people in my family, for talking badly about the different skin tones of African-Americans (list and forgive). Please forgive my family members for ranking folks, within our own race, Lord, in Jesus' name.

Skin color war, leave. Ranking, leave. Jealousy, leave. Anger, leave. Shame, leave. Self-hate, leave. Mockery, leave. Teasing, leave. Self-doubt, leave. Inability to be loved, leave. Competition, leave. Cruelty, leave. Abandonment, leave. Social ranking based on skin color, leave. Depression, leave. Sabotaging ourselves, leave in Jesus' name.

Self-esteem, return. Self-love, return. Ability to laugh at self, return. Ability to laugh with others, return. Love for all of God's creation, return, in Jesus' name.

Lord, please bring unity among African-Americans, where skin tone doesn't matter. Please restore to my family line, peace among our color hues, to me, my children, and my children's children for a thousand generations. In Jesus' name. Amen.

90. STAYING IN YOUR PLACE

Lord, I ask You to please break off the curse of staying in our place, off my family line.

Lord, I cut, break, and sever all ties to the curse of staying in our place off, my family line, in the name of Jesus.

This is a complicated prayer, because You ask us Lord Jesus to be servants to one another. To love one another. To forgive one another.

What You do not ask, is that we exploit one another.
Or put one another down. Or dehumanize one another.

While I understand the old time thinking, that we should stay in our place, it's a new day. That thinking was once important for the preservation of our family, but not anymore.

Lord, grant me the boldness of Christ to speak up when I need to, to do more when I need to, to have courage to challenge the establishment when I need to.

Staying in place, is good when you're a child, but I'm not a child anymore. Following directions is good, when the directions are for my good, but not when they're used to exploit me or my family. Lord, grant me discernment for when to stay in place and when to stand out of place.

Lord, I forgive the people who introduced staying in our place, to our family line. I realize that it was a means of survival, that worked, and sometimes didn't work.

Lord I forgive anyone currently in my family who insists we stay in our place, and not act on Your inspiration. Stepping out, into new areas is hard. But we have to trust You Lord, that when You say move, we need to move!

Lord I give You my fear of stepping out of place. I've been so conditioned to be obedient, that I sometimes ignore Your encouragement.
Please grant me clear understanding of my position in every situation, and tell me the appropriate time to MOVE!

Staying in my place, leave! Shame, leave. Fear, leave. Anger, leave. Guilt, leave. Blame, leave. Lies, leave. Courage, return. Grace, return. Forgiveness, return. Love, return.

Lord, please grant my family the courage, to not stay in their place, from my parents, to me, to my children, and to my children's children, for a thousand generations. Help us to move into anything You have, that's better for us, in Jesus' name. Amen.

91. UNEMPLOYMENT FOR THE FAMILY

Heavenly Father, in the name of Jesus, I ask that You would please remove the curse of unemployment off my family line.

As a member of the our family's line, I cut, sever, and break off all curses of unemployment off my family line.

I humbly apologize to You for any one in my family line (white or black) that brought this curse on our line. I apologize for their actions, and ask that You would please forgive them. I especially ask for forgiveness for slave masters in my family line, who worked their slaves to death.

I choose to forgive all persons, institutions and laws that kept my family shackled to the curse of unemployment.

I choose to forgive every missed career opportunity, missed job, missed opportunity, missed promotion, all demotions, furloughs and firings that my family had to endure in this country.

I choose to forgive all those throughout the decades, who lied, stole, and thwarted my family out of paying positions, for their own personal gain or agendas (list and forgive).

I give You Lord, all inherited emotions tied to unemployment, including frustration, agitation, hopelessness, mistrust, revenge, apathy, laziness, humiliation, diversions, excuses, sadness, shame, despair, guilt, blame, and insecurity. I call them all to LEAVE my family line, in the name of Jesus.

I ask that You would break, my family members' co-dependence on small unemployment checks, welfare checks, lousy compensation, family loans, or friends' handouts.

I pray for help to find good work for my family members, Lord.
I pray for new career paths for my family members, that will use their gifts to Your glory.

Please Lord, bring work that makes their hearts soar when they go to work.
Please Lord, bring work, that gives them pleasure being around the people they work with.
Please Lord, bring work, that serves others for the greater good of their communities.
Please Lord, bring work, that brings dignity and self-satisfaction back to their dinner table.

These things I ask, in Jesus' precious name. Amen

92. UNEMPLOYMENT FOR ME

Since the day we were freed from slavery, Lord, this country has systematically kept us from receiving proper compensation for the work, they used to get from us for free.
In the name of Jesus, I choose to forgive this country for this gross sin.

I cut, sever, and break off all curses of unemployment off me, in the name of Jesus.

I humbly apologize for anyone in my family line, that brought this curse on our line. I apologize for their actions, and ask that You would please forgive them, including the slave masters in my family line that worked their slaves to the point of bringing curses on themselves.

I ask You Lord, to please remove the curse of unemployment off me, in the name of Jesus. I choose to forgive all persons and institutions that have kept my family shackled to the curse of unemployment. I forgive every firing, missed job, and foiled career opportunity.

I choose to forgive all those, who lied, stole, and kept me out of paid positions, for their own personal gain or agendas.

I give You Lord, all my inherited emotions tied to unemployment. Frustration, leave. Anger, leave. Agitation, leave. Hopelessness, leave. Mistrust, leave. Revenge, leave. Laziness, leave. Humiliation, leave. Depressions, leave. Excuses, leave. Sadness, leave. Shame, leave. Despair, leave. Guilt, leave. Blame, leave. Insecurity, leave. Wanting to give up, leave. Unemployment leave, in the name of Jesus.

I ask that You would break, Lord Jesus, all my co-dependence on small wages, welfare checks, lousy compensation, family loans, or friends' handouts.

I pray for employment that will get me to the place where I can take care of myself and my loved ones. I ask You Lord to please remove any blocks that keeps me from a fair and proper job.

Mostly Lord, I pray for work. But not just any work, Lord.
I pray for a blessing in a career where I can use my gifts and talents to Your glory.
May I be able to work in a place where my heart sings when I go to work.
May I be able to work where it's a pleasure to be around the people I work with.
May I work, where I can serve the greater good.
May I work, so I can bring dignity and plenty, back to my dinner table.
May I work, to have enough to share with those in need, remembering how far You've brought me, Lord.
These things I pray for me, my children, and my children's children, for a thousand generations. In Jesus' holy name. Amen

93. UNFAIR EMPLOYERS

Father, in the name of Jesus, I come before Your throne, asking You to please remove off my family line, the curse of having an unfair employer.

I cut, sever, and break off all curses off my family where we endured cruel task masters, who were physically brutal, verbally abusive, and tactically inhumane to our family line, while acquiring free labor from us, as slaves.

I don't know who in my family introduced this curse to our family line, but I humbly ask for their forgiveness. It could have started all the way back in Egypt, or any other African, Asian or European Empire where my ancestors held massive groups of people in slavery. For this Lord, I apologize.

I apologize and repent for our family members (white and black) who were unfair taskmasters or employers, starting from the beginning of my family line.

I apologize for the first person who introduced this curse onto our family line, and I repent and apologize for every person in my family that perpetuated this curse throughout the years, including my living family, myself, or my children.

In the name of Jesus, I choose to forgive all those, who were cruel taskmasters and unfair employers throughout the years. I forgive all physical brutality, verbal abuse, and tactical inhumanity that was done to my family line, including the free labor of slavery.

I choose to forgive all unfair employers throughout my history (list all bad employers, ask God to forgive them, then you forgive them).

Please change the curse of bad employers to a blessing of good employers.

Please, Lord grant us bosses,
who are effective, without humiliating others
who are fair and just, without taking their frustration out on their staff
who, when a problem is not working out, they resolve it, without cruelty
who maintains compassion and reason, in all circumstances.

Lord, please close and seal all spiritual doors, windows, flooring and ceilings in the spiritual realm, and keep the curse of unfair employers off of our lives.

Grant us the ability to see when bosses are being cruel and confront them in the name of Jesus Christ.

Please restore, all that the enemy tried to kill in us during slavery.
Please grant us good employers, who inspire us to do our best. In Jesus' name. Amen.

94. UNFAIR COURT SYSTEMS

Father, in the name of Jesus, I ask that You would please forgive this nation, for its bigotry in its court systems.

From the founding of its courts and laws in the 1600's, to its gradual biasness against blacks and the poor in this nation, all the way to this present day, Lord, I ask that You would forgive and please break the curse of unfair court systems off my family line and off this nation.

Lord, please break the power of unfair court systems, unfair laws, unfair prosecutors, unfair defenders, unfair judges and juries that are prejudice against blacks, women, the poor, and the disenfranchised.

I ask You Lord to please reinstate the original intent of the constitution as it was written with liberty for all people. Please Jesus, reverse the courts systems' biasness in favor of the rich and powerful.

Lord, please remove the curse of unfair court trials and sentencing from our United States' Federal, State and Local court systems. Lord, please remove the curse of all laws that only benefit the rich and powerful in our land. Heavenly Father, please send down Your Holy Court System to reign over our corrupt court systems that land the innocent in jail, and set the guilty free.

Please Lord, cancel the generational curse of incarceration off every family in America, including my own family (if applies).
Please set the captives free, Lord. Not just physically, but mentally, and spiritually, too. Please Lord, heal the minds of former inmates from their past, allowing them to become productive citizens in our world.
Please surround them Lord, with a community of love and compassion.

Lord, please bring those who are truly guilty, just trails, good evident and fair sentencing.

Lord would You please break off the unfair sentencing that blacks have endured since their abductions from Africa. We were bound and incarcerated in prisons without trails, in our native land of Africa, BEFORE we even stepped foot on this land. We were bound and chained and shipped to this country and then, once we landed, we were incarcerated in holding cells, camps and bound again in chains until sold. No trails, Lord. No rights, Lord. That's how <u>we started out</u> in this country, Father God. And You saw it all.

Lord You saw in the beginning of this nation in the 1600s, when freedom and pseudo freedom for blacks began to turn against us, with the highest court ruling, against John Punch, a black man. You saw how the ruling for the two white servants who ran away with John from their master, were only given extended years of free labor, while John Punch received a lifelong sentence of free labor, for the same crime.

Father God, please break that root sentencing of John Punch OFF our judicial system of unfair and harsh sentences against African-Americans.

From the time of the sentencing of John Punch in 1640, I break the curse of unfair court trials and sentencing off African-Americans in the name of Jesus Christ of Nazareth!

On down to the time of 1740, I break the curse of unfair trials and sentencing off African-Americans in the name of Jesus Christ of Nazareth.

On down to the time of 1840, I break the curse of unfair trails and sentencing off African-Americans in the name of Jesus Christ of Nazareth.

On down to the time of 1940, I break the curse of unfair trials and sentencing off African-Americans in the name of Jesus Christ of Nazareth.

On down to the time of 2040 I break the curse of unfair trials and sentencing off African-Americans, to our children, our children's children, for a thousand generations, in the name of Jesus Christ of Nazareth.

Lord, I choose to forgive every police officer, bailiff, prosecutor, defender, judge, jury, prison officer and prison warden that misappropriated their power by false arrests, verdicts, and cruel and unusual punishments, based on their biasness against blacks.
I choose to forgive the beginning of unjust sentencing against blacks, by forgiving the court members and the judge that sentenced John Punch to life, without freedom.

Lord I cut, break, and sever all ties to unfair court systems off my family's life. I choose to forgive any court systems, judges, juries, defenders or prosecutors who falsely arrested, convicted and sentenced my family members (list and forgive).

Lord I ask that You would forgive any member of my family that brought this curse on our family line, and I choose to forgive their actions as well (list and forgive).Lord I ask that You would please break this pattern of incarceration off my family line.

In cases where people get off or receive light sentences for threatening, harming, or killing African-Americans, I pray Lord, that You would please correct the weights of justice and remove the curse of unfair court trails and sentencing of perpetrators who mistreat black people. I pray for Your blessing of fairness in the court systems with police, bailiffs, prosecutors, defenders, judges, juries and laws, for those who are truly guilty of crimes against African-Americans.

Lord Jesus help. This is such a big problem that's come down through the generations of this country.

Lord, it's going to take You, to set it all straight.
It's going to take You to make things right.
It's going to take You to allow true justice to rule.
It's going to take You to heal my broken people.

Lord God, please stop my people from needlessly going to jail.
How we started out in this country, being bound and chained as slaves from the get-go, we now break, in the name of Jesus Christ of Nazareth.
Let our journey in this land, start anew.

Unfair court systems, leave in the name of Jesus Christ.
Incarceration, leave in the name of Jesus.
Chains, leave in the name of Jesus.
Old slavery patterns, leave in the name of Jesus.
Brokenness, leave in the name of Jesus.
Abandonment, leave in the name of Jesus.
Generational patterns of incarceration, leave in the name of Jesus.
Corrupt politicians, leave in the name of Jesus.

Faith in Christ, return in the name of Jesus.
Justice, return in the name of Jesus.
Reparations, come in the name of Jesus.
Mental health, be restored in the name of Jesus.
Healthy families, return in the name of Jesus.
Jobs, return in the name of Jesus.
Education, return in the name of Jesus.
Opportunity, return in the name of Jesus.
Entrepreneurial opportunities, return in the name of Jesus.
Productivity, return in the name of Jesus.
Voting rights for all, return in the name of Jesus.

Please Lord,
No more abductions from our homes, Lord (false arrests).
No more chains Lord (handcuffs).
No more holding cells, Lord (being booked).
No more selling us off, Lord (judges sentencing people to make a profit for facilities).
No more plantations, Lord, (prisons, labor camps).
Set us free, Lord. Please, set us free. In Jesus' holy name. Amen.

Paul L. Cox, *Guidelines to Deliverance*
DVD: *Slavery and the Making of American,* Director Dante J. James
Judge Mark Ciavarella Jr, *"Kids For Cash"* Scandal 2008
www.huffingtonpost.com/2011/08/.../mark-ciavarella-jr_n_924324.html

95. UNFAIR WAGES

Lord, since the day we were freed men and women, and asked for proper compensation for a day's labor, this country has not wanted to pay us for the labor they once got for free. They have systematically kept us and our ancestors from the wages they pay themselves. While some African-Americans throughout the years, have overcome this curse, many of us, have not.

So, Heavenly Father, as a member of my family's line, I cut, sever, and break off all curses of unfair wages off my family line.

I humbly apologize for any and every one in my family (white and black) who brought this curse on our line. I apologize for their actions, and ask that You would please forgive them for what they did, including the slave masters in my family line that worked their slaves to death.

I ask that You would please remove this curse, Lord. I choose to forgive all persons and institutions that have kept my family shackled to the curse of unfair wages, including slavery and sharecropping. I forgive every lack of promotion or raise, every excuse for unequal pay, every stall tactic not to pay our wages, and every foiled career opportunity.

I choose to forgive all those, who lied, stole, and thwarted my family members, out of paying positions, for their own personal gain or agendas.

I give You Lord, all inherited emotions tied to unfair wages, including frustration, anger, agitation, bitterness, hopelessness, mistrust, revenge, apathy, laziness, humiliation, diversions, excuses, sadness, shame, despair, guilt, blame, and insecurity. I call them all to LEAVE off our family line, in the name of Jesus.

As You provided manna for the children of Israel, I pray and thank You for Your provision Lord. Please help our family financially to get to the place where we can take care of ourselves. Whether it's financial aid to go back to school, or assistance to live, or help with child care, please provide us a way to improve our circumstances.

I also pray Lord Jesus, that You would please allow me and my family members the opportunity to break off our dependence on small wages, pay outs, welfare checks, lousy retirement packages, or loans and handouts from family or friends.

Lord, I pray for the blessing of fair wages for all my family members, using the talents and gifts You've given us. May our wages be fair Lord, for me, my children, and my children's children for a thousand generations.
When they aren't fair, please grant us a lion's heart to challenge the system. And if they don't want to pay us a fair wage, please help us find a better job, in Jesus' name. Amen.

96. VANITY

Lord, in the name of Jesus, I come before You, asking that You would please remove all curses of vanity, off my family line.

I break, cut and sever all ties to the curse of vanity off me and my family line, in the name of Jesus Christ of Nazareth.

Lord, I ask that You would please forgive the initiator of this curse on my family line, and I repent for whatever they did, to bring this curse about. I choose to forgive them for their actions, as well as any other family members that have perpetuated this curse, including myself (if applies).

Please forgive me Lord for anything that I have put, above You.

(Figure out what vain or overly proud thing you do, that goes against God's love and ask Him for forgiveness. The following apologies are some examples of what to say.)

Lord, I'm sorry for my superior attitude.
I'm sorry for my racism.
I'm sorry for my critical spirit.
I'm sorry for my judgments of others.
I'm sorry for ridiculing others, especially for things they can't help.
I'm sorry for comparing myself to others.
I'm sorry for laughing at people.
I'm sorry for my anger toward people.
I'm sorry for envying others.
I'm sorry for being jealous of others.
I'm sorry for despising others.
I'm sorry for getting drunk.
I'm sorry for not obeying You, because I'm scared or shamed of my Christianity.
I'm sorry for not listening to Your Spirit, when what You ask of me isn't "cool".
I'm sorry for putting others down, because they aren't cool.
I'm sorry for making myself feel superior to others:
(list everything you believe is better about yourself, than others)
Lord, I'm sorry for believing I'm better than other people, because:
I drive a better car, I live in a better home, I live in a better country, I live in a better neighborhood, I have a better husband or wife, I have a better girlfriend or boyfriend, I have a better job, better education, better summer home, better body, better skin, better shape, better wage, better position, better school for my kids, better church, better playground, better kids, better politics, better ideas, better retirement, better medical insurance, better doctors, better way of life, better anything….compared to "them"!

This is the vanity that You hate Lord, because everything we have, everything we are, is a gift from You. We didn't earn or deserve what we have. All we have, comes from the Living God. Even the very breath we breathe.

Thank You Father God. Thank You Lord Jesus, for all that I have.
Grant me a heart of gratitude.
For vanity only fuels the fire of desire. It never quenches desire's thirst.

Lord, rid me of the curse of vanity.
Help me to be loving, caring, and willing not to mock others, for my own pleasure.

Please forgive me and my family members for our critical spirits.

Vanity, leave. False pride, leave. Insecurity, leave. Anger, leave. Comparisons, leave. Judgments, leave. Envy, leave. Jealousy, leave. Sadness, leave. Rivalry, leave. Criticism, leave. Gossip, leave. Shame, leave. Doubt, leave. In Jesus' name.

God's joy, return. God's pleasure, return. God's love, return. Contentment, return. Sharing, return. Servant hood, return. Gratitude, return in Jesus' name.

Thank You Lord for allowing me to be in my right mind.
Thank You Lord Jesus for saving my soul.
Thank You for my freedom.
Thank You Lord that I woke up this morning.
Thank You Lord that my body works.
Thank You Lord for my family.
Thank You Lord for my home.
Thank You for my car or transportation or legs to walk.
Thank You for my job.
Thank You for my career.
Thank You for my health.
Thank You for my wealth.
Thank You for my position.
Thank You for my ambition.
Thank You for my time.
Thank You for Your time.
Thank You for my reason for living.
Thank You for my loved ones.
Thank You for my future.
Thank You for Your abundance.

Lord Jesus, please keep reminding us, it's not about us. Fill us with Your love. Show us Your way. The best way! To me, to my children, and to my children's children for a thousand generations. In Jesus' name. Amen.

97. VOODOO

Well Lord, some stuff that came over from African, should have stayed in Africa.

Lord God Almighty, in the name of Your Son, Jesus Christ, I humbly ask that You would please remove the curse of voodoo or vodou or vodun or vodoun or vudun, or voudou, or whatever other titles it goes by, OFF my family line, in Jesus' name.

As a member of this family, I cut, break, and sever all ties of voodoo, vodou, vodun, vodoun, vudun, voudou and any other witchcraft OFF my family line, by the power invested in me by the Blood of the Lamb, Jesus Christ of Nazareth.

Break. Break.

Lord Jesus, please break the curse off every generation in my family line, that used voodoo or witchcraft.

Lord, I choose to break off all ties of voodoo off me, my children, my children's children for a thousand generations.

Lord I humbly come before Your throne, asking forgiveness of _all_ of my family members that used voodoo. I know the use of it, is an abomination to You Lord. So I repent for all my family line for using it. (You might need to wait a minute and let the sins of your family fall off. You should say you're sorry over and over for deeds you're not even aware of. Whatever imagery or words come to mind, repent.)

Please forgive all blood sacrifices, heart sacrifices, all chicken and animal sacrifices, children and family sacrifices, soul sacrifices, spiritual sacrifices, material goods sacrifices, life dedications, oaths, bargains, exchanges, all means of witchcraft to try and manipulate God or people to do _our_ bidding. Lord I'm sorry and repent for all sexual sacrifices, all incantations, amulets, dolls, potions, poisons, letters, warnings, postings, hexes, books on spells, spells, moneys paid to witches, moneys for advice on doing evil, moneys for evil purchases, lending our innocent or sanctified spirits over to voodoo, death potions, death traps, lust for death, lust for desire, lust for control.

Please forgive (list family members, what they did, and ask God for their forgiveness)
I repent for our family's use of witch doctors and sorcerers, for social rankings or status positions.

Please forgive us, every time my family members mixed our faith of You with the practice of voodoo.

Please forgive us, Lord of all these actions and please remove the stain of them from our family line, in the name of the Father, the Son and the Holy Ghost.
Lord Jesus, please forgive the person (s) that introduced this curse onto our family. I repent for their sake, and I choose to forgive them. Please forgive every family member who knowingly or unknowingly brought voodoo back into the family line, and please forgive me for any time I knowingly or unknowingly use any form of witchcraft.
I humbly apologize to You Lord God. I'm sorry Lord. Please make me aware when I'm using magic, which hurts You.

I confess to You Lord, that I don't need to control everyone in my life.
You don't even do that, and You're God.
You grant free will.
Help me to trust and lean on the Master of the Universe for my peace and joy.

Lord please cancel and break all spells over me and my family line.
Lord Jesus, please break every evil pattern, sent our way.

Voodoo, vodou, vodun, vodoun, vudun, voudou, leave in the name of Jesus Christ of Nazareth, by the blood He shed on cross.
Pettiness, leave. Anger, leave. Needing to control, leave. Powerlessness, leave. Sadness, leave. Lust, leave. Fear, Leave. Victimization, leave. Jealousy, leave. Envy, leave. Procrastination, leave. Lust for money, leave. Lust for status, leave. Insecurity, leave. Impatience, leave. NOW IN JESUS' NAME!

I give You Lord, the following people that I am mad at, envious of, or lustful for (list, forgive and bless them).

Courage, return. Control over my own life, return. Purpose, return.
Joy, return. Peace, return. Commitment, return. The right focus, return.
The True God return, to my heart, to my mind. to my soul. In Jesus' name.

Lord I choose to forgive anyone outside my family line, for placing any curses, witchcraft or voodoo on my family line.

I break all curses of voodoo that come against us, in the name of Jesus Christ, by His Blood shed on the cross, for the remission of the world's sin.

Have mercy on my enemies, Lord Jesus, because I choose not to partner with the devil. So I send only blessings back to my enemies Lord, in Jesus name.

May they come to know You as their Lord and Savior. In Jesus Christ's name, Amen and Amen.

http://en.wikipedia.org/wiki/West_African_Vodun
http://en.wikipedia.org/wiki/Haitian_Vodou

98. VIOLENCE

Since the founding of this nation, it's been a history of violence. People killing people. People hurting people. And for what?

So Father God, I ask You to please remove the curse of violence off my family line, and off all African-Americans' family lines.

Lord I repent for the person (black or white) in my family line that introduced violence into our family. I ask Lord that You would please forgive them and everyone else who was violent in my family line.

I choose to forgive all those who were violent to my family members throughout history.

I choose to forgive all the violence my family members endured, from the point of history where they were abducted from Africa.
I choose to forgive all the violence my family members endured, in the holding camps and prisons while waiting for their departure to America.
I choose to forgive all the violence my family members endured, crossing the Atlantic, while cramped in slave ships for weeks.
I choose to forgive all the violence my family members endured, being groomed, inspected, grabbed, auctioned, and sold!
I choose to forgive all the violence my family members endured, being slaves:
I choose to forgive every beating, every whipping, every lynching, every branding, every blow to the body, every torture, every burning, every spiking, every castration, every rape, every murder, and every other punishment performed on my family line, during slavery, and after slavery.

As a member of this family line, I cut, break, and sever all ties to the curse of violence, off my family line, whether we were victims or participants.

For every violent incident in the past, that my family members committed,
I repent to You Lord, and apologize (list each family member and the incident, ask God for forgiveness, then you forgive them).

If my house is violent, I repent.
If my street is violent, I repent.
If my neighborhood is violent, I repent.
If my city is violent, I repent.
If my state is violent, I repent.
Lord Jesus, my nation is violent, so I repent.
Please forgive all these violations, in Jesus' name.

Lord, please bring peace to these places, especially in my home.
Please break the violence in my household, Lord Jesus, or help me move out!

Please tell me where I need to repent, Lord, so peace can return to my family line.
Please tell me where I need to repent, Lord, so peace can return to our home, our job,
our relationships, our street, our community center, our schools, our stores, our neighborhoods, our parks, our highways, our malls, our places of worship.

Lord, if we are to live in a society of violence,
what are we to do?
How are we to survive?
We certainly don't want to be victims anymore.

Lord Jesus, I ask that the protection of the Holy Spirit be around us.
I ask that You Lord Jesus would protect us night and day, 24 hours a day.
I give You our fear.
I give You our need to be violent.
I give You our rage.
I give You our powerlessness.
I give You our rash decisions.
I give You our greed.
I give You our pride.
I give You our selfishness.
I give You our inability to forgive.
I give You our grudges.
I give You our stress.
I give You our self-destruction.
I give You our pranks that lead to violence.
I give You our frustration.
I give You our shame.
I give You our guilt.
I give You our insecurities.
I give You our lack of self control.
I give You our need to retaliate.
I give You our tempers.
I give You our need to control the situation, instead of giving the situation to You.

Revenge, leave.
Anger, leave.
Being violent, leave.
Being a victim, leave.

Serenity, return.
Goodwill, return.
Loving Community, return.
Joy, return.
Love, return.
Safety, return. In Jesus' name. Amen.

99. WOMEN HANGING ON YOUR MAN

Father, in the name of Jesus, we have a problem. There are women, who constantly get up under my man.

So first and foremost, in the name of Jesus, I humbly come before Your throne Lord, asking You to please remove the curse of women hanging on my man, off me and my family line.

By the power of Jesus Christ, I cut, break and sever all ties to the curse of women continuously throwing themselves on our men, off me and my family line.

I apologize and ask You Lord to please forgive all the women in my family line that brought on this curse, by throwing themselves on men or stealing men away from their significant others.

I apologize Lord for every man in my family line that brought on this curse by throwing themselves on women or stealing women away from their significant others.

I humbly apologize every time I knowingly and unknowingly flirted with men I shouldn't have. I'm sorry God and I repent for perpetuating this curse.

Please cleanse this curse off my family line, and restore all that's decent and proper.
Lord, let the phone calls stop.
Lord, let the text messaging stop.
Lord, let the touching, whether proper or improper, stop.
Lord, let the silent glances and smiles, stop.
Lord, let all indecent and improper contact, whether verbal, written, or physical, stop, in the name of Jesus.

Please Lord, I choose to give You my anger is this situation (list all events and forgive).
I choose to forgive my man for encouraging it, voluntarily or involuntarily.
I choose to forgive every woman that's been up under him (list and forgive).
I give You my bitterness in these situations.
I give You my insecurity and vulnerability in these situations.
I give You my outrage and ignorance in these situations.
I give You the woman I've turned into, as opposed to the woman I want to be, Lord.

Help Lord.
My man's insecurities in himself, have turned me into a shrew.
If this relationship _is_ of You, please mend it, Lord.
Show me how to be the loving woman You want me to be to him.
If this relationship _is not_ of You, then give me the strength to break it off and let him go! In Jesus' name. Amen!

100. THE BLESSING OF CONQUERING OUR ENEMIES

Lord, in establishing this country, You showed us that we don't have to use our enemies' rules of engagement, to fight them.

You blessed the people of this nation with vision for new ways to conquer their enemies.

Lord, I come before You,
asking that You would please grant me and my family line,
this country's blessing of conquering our enemies.

Please Lord, grant us
the same wisdom You gave George Washington to run the Revolutionary War,
the same faith to pray to You for guidance,
the same fortitude to lead the battles,
the same humbleness to admit when we feel defeated,
the same courage to defend new strategies,
the same ability to hold our troops together,
the same vision to look down the road,
and know that what we're fighting for, is worth it.

Help my opponents to underestimate me.
Help me not to fall into the trap of being defined by my opponents.
Help me not to give up, even when it looks like all is lost.
Help me not to give up, even when my opponent is asking for my surrender.

What looks like impossible, is possible with You, Lord.

When it looks like I'm too weak and my opponents are too strong,
help me Lord to remember that You have the last say in every battle.

I claim this nation's blessing of the underdog,
which won us the Revolutionary War against the British;
a war we never should have won,
being they were the most powerful nation in the world.

I claim the Founding Fathers' blessing of persuasion,
with the ability to encourage my team,
not with money,
but by the principles for which we are fighting.

I claim the Continental Army's blessing of using the element of surprise,
so we are able to turn the events of our opponents, to our favor.

I claim the Constitution's blessing of motivating my team
to claim our God-given rights to freedom and justice for ourselves and our families.

When committees tie up resources,
I pray Lord, You would give us what we need
in order to see the victory through to the end.

I pray You would please be
our Supplier,
our Provider,
our Protector, and
our Guide through these trying times, Lord.

Like George Washington, please grant me Lord the ability to hold my team
together, despite the deficits, distractions, hardships, distrusts, defeats and fall outs.

Please grant me a clear vision of what You want me to share with my team
and how to execute that vision to the team at large.

If it is Your will Lord, establish in me, as You did with the Founding Fathers,
a new beginning,
a new plan of action,
and a new purpose for liberty.

May we become, a new race of men and women in this country,
as those that fought together in the Revolutionary War.

Together those citizens,
black and white,
male and female,
young and old,
overcame the greatest military power in the world,
for the purpose of freedom
for all!

Please Lord,
guide our feet,
influence our minds,
open our hearts,
endow us with Your wisdom and compassion,

as we move forward to create a world that affirms the dignity of every human being,
in Jesus' holy name. Amen!

DVD: *Liberty! The American Revolution*, Director Ellen Hovde and Director Muffie Meyer

Pamela Burgess Main has a Bachelor of Arts in Cinema and Television Production from the University of Southern California, as well as a Master of Arts in Theology from Fuller Theological Seminary. She has been involved in inner city and suburban ministry for over 25 years.